STEADFASTNESS OF THE SAINTS

*A Journal of Peace and War
in Central and North America*

DANIEL BERRIGAN

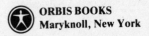
ORBIS BOOKS
Maryknoll, New York

DOVE COMMUNICATIONS
Melbourne, Australia

The Catholic Foreign Mission Society of America (Maryknoll) recruits and trains people for overseas missionary service. Through Orbis Books Maryknoll aims to foster the international dialogue that is essential to mission. The books published, however, reflect the opinions of their authors and are not meant to represent the official position of the society.

Copyright © 1985 by Daniel Berrigan
Published in the United States of America by Orbis Books,
Maryknoll, NY 10545
All rights reserved
Manufactured in the United States of America

The photographs between pages 73 and 74 were taken by Dennis Leder

Manuscript editor: William Schlau

Library of Congress Cataloging in Publication Data
Berrigan, Daniel.
  Steadfastness of the saints.

  1. Berrigan, Daniel. 2. Christianity—El Salvador.
3. Christianity—Nicaragua. 4. El Salvador—Politics
and government—1979- . 5. Nicaragua—Politics
and government—1979- . I. Title.
BX4705.B3845B47 1985   282'.7284   85-5120
ISBN 0-88344-447-X (pbk.)

Published in Australia in 1985 by Dove Communications, Box 316 Blackburn, Victoria 3130
Dove ISBN 0-85924-388-5

Contents

Foreword v

Departure 1

El Salvador 6

Hymn to the New Humanity 74

Nicaragua 77

Envoi 130

To those who profess and pay up—
   the wielders of hammers
   and pourers of blood.
Swords into plowshares,
   fury into beatitude.

Foreword

An early inspiration of Ignatius Loyola was to keep his fledgling society united through frequent letters. No sooner had his small band of "companions of Jesus" offered their talents for the service of the church than they were quickly missioned to distant points. They departed with a promise to keep one another informed. Today, many Jesuit archives attest to how seriously that contract was honored.

Like numerous sparks of saintly wisdom, when routinized, correspondence can lose its fire too. Letters become disimpassioned or formulas for instruction. The conditions that once prompted Jesuits to seek fraternal solace or the assurance of collective unity become conditions, in a comfortable society, that prompt piety and abstractions. No further need to explain why a letter from Jesuits that stands out for its urgency is apt to quickly ignite their brothers' concern,

In today's peril, a letter originating in Central America can be expected to have little else but urgency. Two such letters were tacked on the bulletin board of my home community, greeting my return from a precarious Christmas spent on Nicaraguan soil in the war zone near the Honduran border. One letter was from the Jesuit provincial superior of Central America to his North American colleagues; the other was directed from the superiors of Central America to all U.S. Jesuits.

The letters spoke sobering words of a deteriorated situation in Central America, of a civil war that "could take on proportions which are unsuspected even at this moment," of the danger of "a regional war with enormous costs to human life." One letter urged Jesuits "to contribute according to your possibilities," and concluded: "For the love of God, help us to prevent war so that in the difficult search for freedom and justice our peoples are not obliged to continue shedding their blood."

The power of these messages was compounded by firsthand experience of the sufferings in Central America. A return letter seemed essential, but somehow inadequate. How does a U.S. citizen and a Jesuit respond, knowing of U.S. supported aggression against people with whom his fellow Jesuits live and work? Surely this quandary could not be solved by beleaguered brothers in El Salvador or Nicaragua; it begged a discussion closer to home.

I was—and am—thankful a fellow Jesuit and dear friend has been seasoned in such complexities; I contacted my brother Dan. He too had written to the provincial, felt the poignancy of the letters, and was searching for a more tangible response. From him a most simple and logical plan soon emerged: to go, to learn from, to be with the suffering people near our border. A spark of saintly wisdom!

Among the many emotions that marked our travels, one emerges for me as the most informative and lasting. It is gratitude—for again knowing the untold power of simple presence; for being with people of hope who become such out of persecution; and, not least of all, for my fellow travelers whose own gratitude for life is clear in word and deed.

It was a special blessing to have a companion as durable as Dan. He is the rarest of Jesuits, an endangered species, adventurous in spirit and critical in mind, irreverent toward the powers yet filled with ultimate concern. With his humor and insight and patient endurance, we not only weathered much but turned all into gain.

Our odyssey, as readers will here discover, was both modest and urgent. A gesture at keeping informed, of intensifying communication between Jesuits and friends in the north and those in the south. Its graced moments were many, leading us to a rare convergence of Soul. And through that common meeting of struggle and faith, our individual journeys continue forward, in hope: *Adelante, siempre adelante!*

DENNIS LEDER, S.J.

1
Departure

News of the proposed voyage was variously received.
Someone asked half humorously, half in exasperation, "Why Central America? Isn't there enough excitement for your turbulent spirit right here in New York?"
The question was loaded, as we both knew. I had something quite different in mind—as we both knew.
Others probed the matter of fear. Wasn't I afraid? Wasn't I aware that I was putting myself in considerable danger?
I thought awhile. "As to the first question, not really." (And how does one explain the *absence* of fear?) "As to the second, of course; what fool wouldn't be?"

•

Something different in mind; convergences, analogies, a nudge in the night. It tells me: a trip to Central America won't be anything like going to another planet. Nothing wonderful and strange.
After the U.S.? It will be, must be, a recognition scene. Good people in trouble, power-mad authority calling the shots.
Or something else: the attempt of a new government to survive, to pick up the pieces of lives, communities, institutions; to be a vessel of hope for people long tossed aside, betrayed, preyed upon.

•

The night before departure we broke bread, passed the cup. We have no better rite of passage, under whatever circumstance.

We prayed not only for ourselves: safe exodus, safe return. But for all those in prison, there, here, everywhere. For the Plowshare folk in Florida and Syracuse. For all who wage peace, oppose violence, and pay up.

Speaking of which, and speaking as well of passing the cup, the week previous, in Syracuse, I was allowed to take the stand at a trial—a rare concession indeed. I was asked to explain the symbolism of the blood (their own) which the defendants had poured on the bomber at Griffiss Air Force Base nearby. Said in part:

—That in the U.S., there are two classic ways of looking at law and conscience. The first is the commonly acceptable one; history has validated it. Which is to say: one is free to shed others' blood in the sanctioned violence called war; and, inevitably, to be honored for valor.

—And the second way, far from acceptable, is summed up in the criminal charges of this trial; one gives one's blood, and is criminalized for the act—as in the present and pressing instance, the Plowshares actions.

—But as to the choice between these two, we have a command issued from the heart of our worship: "My blood, given for you. Do this in memory of Me."

Thus far fear.

•

In February, dutiful citizen and foreseeing, I applied for passport renewal. Alas and alack, after being mailed, the passport turned up missing, for almost three months. Then all of a sudden, it was found, almost as mysteriously. Since it had never been lost, as subsequently was learned, the question arose: How could it be found?

The question, for all its logic, was beside the point. A "hold" had been put on the passport in some mysterious warren of power, where citizenship gets CAT scanned in the dark, and credentials for further existence are issued—or denied.

With three days to go before departure, the holding fist let go. But how come this harmless cleric gets stuck, like an impeding embolism, in the arteries of power?

DEPARTURE

•

Being transplanted, like a tree or a plant, one's leaves wither and droop for a time. The roots pant, desiccated in the open air. They take hold again slowly, slowly. One doesn't expect to cast up a passionflower overnight!
I tell myself this, brace myself for a dry season.

•

We're off and up, Dennis, Gene, and I in this lumbering grand piano. Like a family of circus freaks, shot for the hundredth time from a cannon.
And the motto of the trip just came to me. To wit: Let's test this thing called "soul."
Likewise the question of the trip, in various forms: Does blood run north or south? Whose death is everyone's (or nearly everyone's) death? Who dies first, the gunman or the victim?

•

Dennis, my ever-ready shockproof friend, is also an artist. The "also" is of course redundant as the name of a name; he's an artist. On the plane to Miami, I meet another artist from Brooklyn, off to Nicaragua to see his daughter. His splendid Plowshares woodcut graces my kitchen wall at home. And on the plane, he presents me with a big button he designed—three artists' faces yelling through their paint and brushes: "ARTISTS' CALL AGAINST U.S. INTERVENTION IN CENTRAL AMERICA." These are propitious signs indeed.

•

Into sunlight that strikes one blind.
Into terror. Into gun sights and the pits of gun barrels of the killers for whom killing is a momentary break from boredom.
I came because I wanted to learn from strangers, from Jesuits

and peasants and students and anyone who would tell me how one lives with death. It was as simple as this.

•

But first—Miami, Florida. The longest, biggest death row in the nation. Murder and orange juice and Disney World. (Robert Sullivan, murdered in November, after ten years on death row, pray for us.)

The sinking feeling in my guts as we pass through this spoiled cornucopia, Miami airport. Three cheers for consumerism, free enterprise, the flag above all! Even the young women huckstering Moon's salvation have a tanned, cloned look. Easeful death in the air, miles of smiles. Booths, stores, a half mile of Appetite Row, like neon illumined dentures.

Death? I know, as one knows only in the viscera; what renders me thoughtful, what slows the steps, is by no means fear of our destination; it has everything to do with the U.S.

Do we know ourselves best at the edge of experience, where one is apt, given the world, to be tipped over into the void?

Is Miami the edge of the U.S., or the void?

In any case, an old sense returns: leaving Western Europe for Czechoslovakia and southern Africa in 1965. A like sense, leaving New York for Hanoi in 1968. A sense weirdly akin, leaving for Catonsville in May of that year, leaving for trial in October. Leaving Cornell to dive underground in 1970. Stepping off the edge of the world, the terrain underfoot, the landmarks, seamarks. Leaving for prison; leaving prison, landing safe, even somewhat sane, back in the U.S. Then leaving the community for the Pentagon, again and again—and again: ten, twelve years of leavetaking. The sense beneath the senselessness; that obscure signal, no larger than the flare of a match; enough light for the next step, one only step.

That bitter leavetaking, departing for King of Prussia, 1980. The daunting question, What will come of this? yielding before the simple imperative, sharp as a drumbeat or the beat of a heart not one's own: This is to be done! And all eventualities, like the impeding tails of a kite, flung to the winds; the action is aloft!

Life is, maybe, a series of little deaths? One of the lawyers warned at the time of King of Prussia, "No one will walk away from this!"

Thus for lawyers and their prognostications.

After a time, everyone walked away from what they had, with many a dry throat, walked toward. And all of us still at large, and still unrehabilitated, still on our feet.

2
El Salvador

And so for the first time ever, stepped on Salvador's soil. Gingerly, mindful eyes in the back of one's head. Remembering the American nuns, how their fate, in smoked glasses and plainclothes, geared up here, in this classy refurbished airport: neon, glass, consumerism, mini-Miami.

•

A cusped volcano loomed above, as we came in. The world has blown its top. . . .

•

Stocktaking. If any quality of temperament fits me for these weeks, it's a listening attitude. I can summon a soul struck dumb, willing to spend some 90 percent of the day hearkening to others, the remaining time reflecting, questioning, without hard-nosed judgment, trying the truth for size.

•

San Salvador; we came in search of the Jesuits. In a sense, the start of the trip was its end. Valentín Menendez, provincial superior of Central America; Ignacio Ellacuría, president of the university; John Cortina and Esteban Velásquez, most unacademic scholars; the theologian Jon Sobrino.

Appointments were arranged with each. We found them guarded, courteous, weary; yet each was marked by the "inner light." A look of endurance, of those under siege (bombs, death threats, the violent deaths of those near and dear). Scholars of international stature. Then an added something, born of hope long delayed and of courage, of the solidarity in suffering that lightens the burden. The will to stand and be counted.

Had any other Jesuits, anywhere in the world, lived so long under such severe stress? I doubted it. A decade ago, their house adjoining the campus had been left unprotected; evidently none of them sensed how badly things were tending. Someone climbed the surrounding wall and bombed the house. A metal netting was thereupon strung atop the wall. Someone ingeniously cut through, entered the house and left a bomb. . . .

•

With the provincial, we discussed the controversy that had broken out between the Nicaraguan bishops and the Jesuits. (A recent letter of the bishops urged "dialogue with all sides," including presumably the Somozans, former members of the notorious National Guard. These had escaped prosecution for their crimes, fled the country, and took up arms, joining the "contra" squads who were ravaging northern Nicaragua.)

Menendez, as superior of Central America, was answerable for the Jesuits' response, which had been issued just prior to our arrival. He spoke calmly (everyone here seems to master a kind of intense calm, the surface tension of the storm beneath):

> We had to speak up, or as our letter says, the gospel as well as the writings of recent popes stress that there can be no reconciliation if justice is violated. . . . In our instance, it is simply unthinkable that those who had acted criminally in the recent past, and whose criminal conduct continues to this day in Nicaragua—that these should automatically become party to "national reconciliation." What sort of reconciliation would be possible in such a case? For the conduct of these men is aimed at the destruction of the new government, and the restoration of Somozan authority, aided and abetted by the U.S.

•

Father Ellacuría: "At one time, according to [former Superior General] Arrupe, we of El Salvador were one of the most divided national groups in the society. Now we are one of the most united. It was the deaths of Romero and [Jesuit] Rutilio Grande and the others that turned us around."

•

With Fr. John Cortina we went to San Rocco church for liturgy. A church and a liturgy like few others on earth.

We drove through an urban barrio. Then a sight which—even though one's mind grows blank before the diorama of world misery—this sight all but stopped the heart. We drove up beside a great raw shell of a building, a building of noble proportion and parts. The lower portion was finished and floored over, the upper reaches (the main area that was to have been the sanctuary) open to sky and weather.

Into this shell, like the empty egg of creation, fled the endangered living: children, women, old people. Some to be born there, some to die, most to simply exist. They came from all parts of the war zone, campesinos for the most part, as one would judge from the faces. Many on death lists, many with relatives already disappeared.

They converged and occupied the church, these strange squatters. As far as we could learn, no one, except the newly dead, had departed the premises in the three years since they arrived.

Though we were expected, the door was guarded, and opened to us guardedly. Downstairs, in a vast, badly lit space, the accoutrements of bare existence were scattered about: concrete tanks to catch rain water, privies, clothes lines, cooking fires, hammocks where infants mewed and slept; and in the midst an altar table and benches arranged for worship. They were singing hymns as we came in. I cannot well describe the effect of those voices. There flashed into mind the scene from the *Purgatorio,* souls (and bodies) being purified in a furnace of fire. In their midst, Dante writes, he himself stood, joining in the fabulous dance and singing the praises of God.

What the souls could not know, in the nature of things, was that they stood on the threshhold of the beatific vision, their torment strangely mingled with ecstasy. . . .

We came in, and eventually the people assembled, in no particular order, and yet in a quiet that betokened something of import, some pause, relief in midst of crowding, noise, uncertainty. . . .

I saw young mothers with infants at breast, old men and women, the middle aged. And here, as everywhere, the virtual absence of young men, presumably dead or disappeared or fled to the guerrillas.

The service got underway.

In the pauses between readings from scripture, people took up their songs in the nasal tone, typical, reminiscent in my ear of the atonal chants of north Africa or the keening of the Irish. A whine of supplication and anguish, by no means pleasant to the ear, hardly in unison. And still, how consonant with the long susurration of sorrow here, the surveillance, the danger always pending. I noted that before the service began, Cortina sat a little apart, vigorously scribbling notes; as I presumed, in preparation for the homily to follow. Nothing of the kind. After the Gospel was read, he began what appeared to be a series of reports. He was heard with rapt, painful attention on the part of all. And I began to understand: the ritual included the news of their home villages, news officially proscribed, the battles, deaths, the fortunes of war.

Cortina finished; he was questioned vigorously on this or that point. Only then, when the internees were satisfied, the second Jesuit, Velásquez, undertook the homily. Communion time came. The concentrated lanky figure of Cortina, the muttered "Body of Christ." A clue to survival, mine and theirs, the clue as frail as the wafer melting on a campesino's tongue, or mine. Would we make it, he and I? and my friends, on trial and in prison? We had no guarantee, not one of us; we had only this clue, and a call. After communion, Cortina interpolated another strange moment; he took his notes in hand and held them, one by one, to the candle flame. The papers went up in smoke, and he stamped the embers underfoot. I realized he could not safely leave the premises with such evidence on his person.

We said our farewells, at length. Cortina hovered over us, suddenly grew urgent: Did we want to ride homeward with him? If so, on the *qui vive!* We piled into the pickup. A mile or two down the road he careened to a stop, pulled over. We must find our way home. He had a meeting to attend—alone.

•

We passed two nights in Florida Guest House. Five dollars per night, no cover, entertainment including hours of Eddie Duchin and other impressarios of the fifties. Music to chew gum by.

•

A Swiss nurse, Josyane Sechaud, offered to accompany us to St. Tecla, a camp of the displaced on the city's edge. A third world version, indeed, of what we refer to as inner-city reality. Celestial Jerusalem? This scene had been regurgitated by hell.

Under the burning sun, the burning bald clay, a scenario of utter misery. Shacks of matchwood, caricatures of children; and in the crepuscular light of the interiors, old men, women, infants, crouching somnolent and spiritless, like hopeless prisoners anywhere in the mad world.

There was a single spigot of water for nine hundred people. We saw, piled against the north fence of the camp, a mountain of boxlike concrete objects: sinks, we were informed, for personal hygiene or washing laundry. Sent, in consequence of a visit, by the wife of the chief of state. But they lay there in the noon, hindmost and foremost and to one side, a heap of inspired useless junk. Since there was no water supply, and no disposition to install adequate plumbing, the gifts were meaningless.

It was an image of goodness gone wrong, the gift that comes to nothing. Or of the wealthy, fervent after good works, well intentioned, "going down to the poor."

•

Returning to the city by bus, a tire blew. Everyone blanched and ducked under seats, as though at a burst of gunfire. Then as people gathered their wits and sat upright, the bus coughed and started up again. There were a few nervous laughs.

•

Even the most carefree mortal could sense that the atmosphere in San Salvador is charged with sinister, even bizarre danger. The human off the tracks. You look in the faces of soldiers in the street, and you know it: life is cheaper than the bullet that could end it. No one looks directly at strangers, those who might be called in another time and place (another theology?) one another.

The above is rendered ironically immediate by an event yesterday. We returned late, and commenced to search out the dwelling of a newsman who had offered us lodging for a few nights. It was midnight; the street was like a graveyard lit by fireflies. The three of us separated, searching up and down the street for our elusive house number. It seems that Gene, at some distance, was making progress, in rapid-fire converse with someone. Our new acquaintance was toting a machine gun; it further developed that he was guarding the premises next-door to ours. Who the neighbors were and what their work was and from whence they came—such questions came together as parts of a puzzle; the puzzle, once bonded, could be called a horrid piece of art; the bond being blood.

The following day revealed a pattern. Our neighbors drove in and out of their guarded acres in a huge Cherokee van, its windows tinted black.

We were to see these vehicles frequently, nosing about in traffic, ominous and swift as sharks on the prowl. The death squads, on our street; as we were informed, ten Cuban-American "advisors." A snub-nosed cruiser, ugly, all chrome and class, all but armor-plated; the interior with its occupations and preoccupations, invisible; no glimpse even of a set of brows or of weaponry or a blurred terrorized captive.

•

We saw a Cherokee flash by as we descended from the headquarters of the Mothers of the Disappeared. The sight was enough to set Gene cursing. We arrived at the headquarters, unfortunately too late to take part in a demonstration.

Seventy-five or a hundred of the relatives were crowded into a stifling little room, one of a series of offices above a storefront. All were chattering volubly, relief was in the air. A demonstration had occurred, under the eyes of the death squads, the national police, the local police, the plainclothes police—the unaccountable anonymous army, at war with its own people.

A group of the mothers was clustered about a TV set; their demonstration was part of the day's news. A new order of things. The mothers were no longer to be brutalized; their activities could now be publicly known. (And on a later occasion, Duarte himself would appear with them to endorse their cause.)

And absolutely nothing of substance would occur, nothing would change. There might be, from month to month, a slight dip in the statistics of terror (the government figures being, as the Human Rights Commission insisted, designedly inaccurate).

And apart from issuing the numbers of the dead, as one of the mothers explained, little could be done; by way of legal recourse, nothing. Still, they did what they could; they kept accounts. And this persistence of theirs, this filing of names and numbers and descriptions and places and times—all this dry summation of horror and bloodshed, this was a work of enormous import. Toward accountability. Toward a day, as has been shown in Argentina, that is not delayed forever.

Meantime, too, the figures they issue month after month reprove the official claims, say in effect that no significant letup has occurred since Duarte's election.

On the whitewashed wall, another irony, a poster. It quotes Duarte's oxymoronic dictum: "Our election is a dialogue for peace." Beneath, a multitude of upraised arms and hands, no faces. And the question: "And where will the fifty thousand disappeared Salvadorans cast their vote?"

Hands, arms, no faces. And the numbers stared at us from the blackboard. So many hundreds killed, disappeared, in April,

May, the six months previous; a war tally, a body count; but with a difference. These figures standing, not for a day's score of havoc wrought on an enemy. This is the arithmetic of a new war: abstract emblems of domestic murder, the northern giant nicely meshed with the power politics, the settling of scores of the south, a marriage of blood and technology (sten guns, Cherokees, the technique of torture).

A war on everyone. Also an ecumenical war. Big Brother learns the usefulness of Little Brother, his surrogate bully; the uses of terms like "human rights," "police accountability," "land reform," a code language that translates up north into spasm and overflow the the full bucket, the bottomless well.

Duarte learned, in the school of hard knocks and Byzantine reversals, the uses of such chatter, winning the attention of benign Yankee legislators, minds nodding in consonance: "It's taken some doing, but after all they're getting things under control down there. . . ." The new collaborative colonization is underway. But whose world is it, whose Salvador? And according to whom? Duarte knows. He can address such questions (at once impertinent and pressing, given the Abounding Bucket) in an accent that would charm the cicadas; Notre Dame twang, Spanish lilt.

It remains of little moment, as he knows, that his language corresponds to little of reality in Salvador. Only to a useful, minimal degree. To the degree, say that the language of keepers of a madhouse or a death row could be thought apt to convey the lives and deaths of their victims.

We stood there among the mothers, confounded, put to silence. Their vitality, the delight they showed at being admitted, after so long a time, to the sanctum of the TV news; a more or less tacit admission that "after all, and with necesary distinctions, these campesina women do have a point, so let us allow them to make it in public. And yes, as a further point of honor and proof of change, let the public now learn thay they exist."

They milled about us; they looked blindly beyond us—toward the tube, that tardy credential. Or they animatedly buzzed and gesticulated, presumably in relief. No one, after all, had been brutalized that morning; they had all returned to headquarters safely. The excitement was a kind of Latin outburst of absolute relief. In certain circumstances, not to be murdered must be counted a considerable blessing, a lagniappe even, when the outcome of such actions as these might well be—what it had not been. Therefore, praise.

Gene came through the throng with a suggestion. Might I not address a few words to the group?

About what? I inquired, bewildered.

About anything, came the unhelpful answer.

Well then, let me try. They were disconcertingly attentive, on the spot. Was it the sight of gringo faces in their midst, a hint of support, someone from quarters unexpected, come to lend hand or voice? I could only do what I could. Began by saying, had we known, we would surely have joined their demonstration that morning; alas we were new in their country and had arrived at their office on so fateful a day, only by chance. How I had been part of so many similar demonstrations, for like causes, in so many countries. The most striking being our meetings with the relatives and mothers in Northern Ireland during the prisoners' hunger strike. How we were refused admission to Long Kesh prison, though Bobby Sands, then dying, had sent an urgent request to visit him. How, denied entrance, we resolved to vigil at the gates of the prison, and there began to recite the litany of all the imprisoned, hundreds of them; and after each name, responded in unison: You are not alone!

•

> The church is the voice of the voiceless.
> These silent ones, still
>   they reflect deeply on what they see;
>   in them is humanity's hope.
> Their lives proclaim,
> "You will not take my dignity from me.
> We know that God is choosing the poor
>   as the seed of new life. . . ."
> The church is called to identify with these,
>   to help their faith, hope, and love mature,"
>   to accompany them
>   in their task of making history.
>
>   Enrique Angelelli
>   + **1976**

The upturned faces ravaged with grief; the poor of the Beatitudes; and then the "preferential option," that incalculable shift in the church, signaling the overthrow of the principalities and powers.

They listened, as though for all the world one priest were adding a strand to a life line, joining them to—what? Something beyond ravines and dumps and city morgues and the muffled cries of the tortured, something beyond the nightmares that lay so heavy on their days. I saw in those faces something one seldom sees in such times, whether at home or abroad: even a person from the U.S. can convey hope.

We were invited into an adjoining room, there, in a quieter setting, to question the relatives. Two young women joined us, delegated to speak for the others. They recounted—in a Greek choral way, one threading the other, commenting and enlarging—how Archbishop Romero had been the inspiration of the mothers' group, when it became clear that the Duarte government, in a previous incarnation, would do exactly nothing by way of achieving justice—either for the victims or their families.

How the work had gone forward somehow, in spite of the murder of Marianella Villas, their president. Her body having turned up, after torture and rape, in the San Salvador morgue. How a great outcry arose at her death, she being so well known and loved. Moreover, questions were raised from all sides, since she was killed in the midst of inquiries into the use of phosphorus and napalm by the Salvadoran army.

And all the while, as the two women went on in their gentle tones, I saw out of the corner of my eye, those diminutive mothers drifting in and out of the room. And after a time, I began to understand: they were in turn being interviewed by a staff member, compiling current statistics of the disappeared. And after each interview, the mother would invariably walk to the far end of the table, to a heap of photo albums laid there. Would take one of them in hand, gravely turn page after page; these images out of the national abattoir, the tortured, raped, amputated. The photos that stood horrid surrogate for the young men, absent from streets and homes and churches and factories. The disappeared generation. I could scarcely bear to look at the faces that dared look at such images, and not be turned to stone. How much can one bear?

I did not know. But I sensed that the measure of what could be borne would be revealed neither by psychiatrist nor politician nor bishop. I must go in humility to these unknown, despised lives, upon whom there rested the preferential option of God.

I saw the children and grandchildren clinging to the women; some among the children were stealing glances at the horrid albums. How can this be? I cried in my heart. I saw that monstrous abstraction, the mystery of evil, aiming its arrows at these faces of six or ten years. The children, the not-yet-disappeared. Was this a calling befitting them, that they should be marked, like a too thick set of forest, for destruction? And more: should they see their horrid future in the eyes of the dead?

The mystery of evil. I thought, despite all, it were better named the mystery of hope.

Otherwise we name the mystery as the world names it. It being the world's ploy to name reality in its own favor, according to its own norms. And in so doing, to persuade the church to take up an argument on its terms, those of the world. Why indeed evil, if God is good?

The question is posed by the friends of Job, not by Job.

But whose part should the church take, Job or his friends? The answer is disconcertingly clear; the church should respond with Job, not only against the worldly, but against their language. Hope on, against hope even; since despite all, God is good.

I saw hope in the eyes of the mothers. And I knew, as I have known before, that God is the very Spirit of hope. Further, it matters little to me that I constantly borrow, lay claim to the hope of others. What else but hope, I ask my soul, can respond to omnipresent, violent claimant death?

I sensed that the women were not stalemated by death. They did not apply to death a final (and finally useless) term like "evil." They had other resources; so they could offer another response, even when death seized on them, in its most terrible guise.

They simply hoped on. Their hope was a matter of visibility and danger. It was as tactile as the steps they had ventured that morning, in a forbidden direction.

Likewise, for others in the room a lesser courage was required, nonetheless real. They had come to this place, climbed these stairs, under surveillance; the Cherokee, all-seeing and powerful, lurking by. "Many of those who have lost relatives do not come at all," said one of the staff. "It demands a special bravery to come near this place."

I gained a sense too (in the manner of an examination of conscience) why we of the north are insular and befuddled and rave into the wind our illusions: free world, holding the line, Marxists to the north of us, Marxists to the south. . . .

I would return north, chastened in wariness and compassion, the words of Christ resonating, as though spoken to our church, our military, our culture: "I have compassion on the multitudes, they are as sheep without a shepherd."

My own people, in spite of all. If I could claim an advantage, it was due to nothing on my part, a pure gift: to be enabled to stand among the dispossessed and victimized of the earth. To stand there consciously, a citizen of the U.S., the stigma of our wars and incursions and racism on me. To stand in shame and borrowed hope. So to return.

•

How strange that every scene my eyes light on, however shocking or febrile, is in the nature of a recognition scene. In 1968 I returned from Hanoi, having undergone, in the besieged city, Mr. Johnson's retaliation for the Tet uprising in the south. A friend and I had gone "to the enemy" to receive three released U.S. pilots and accompany them homeward. But the peacemakers were cheated of their prey, as U.S. officials ("under orders from the White House," as they informed us) seized the airmen in Bangkok, sent them home in a bomber. Chagrined, empty-handed, we continued on our way, as best we might. And I wrote a poem en route:

> If I were Pablo Neruda
> or William Blake
> I could bear, and be eloquent
>
> an American name in the world
> where others perish
> in our two murderous hands.

> Alas Berrigan
> you must open these hands
> and see, stigmatized in their palms
> the broken faces
> you yearn toward.
>
> You cannot offer
> being powerless as a woman
> under the rain of fire—
> life, the cover of your body.
>
> Only the innocent die.
> Take up, take up
> the bloody map of the century.
> The long trek homeward begins
> into the land of unknowing.

So it went, and so it goes.

But does "land of unknowing" describe our predicament? A decade of illusion, a decade of delusion. My friends and I walk a thin line indeed, a line which might even be honored by the name vocation, a line like a strung wire, a high wire. We take our lead, as to survival, from those who walk the wire before us, and beckon us on. Mothers on a high wire, campesinos, the poor of the world? All of these. And then, walking ahead of them and us, the "cloud of witnesses," those who have perished, and risen again.

Keeping one's balance. The phrase must be revised: keeping our balance. This has been true under the testing of the years, for so long that it has the iron force of an adage; I would by now be mad north by northeast, mad as the spectacle of brinksmanship, waste, and delusion of America—but for my friends and family, who encompass all I can muster of faith and hope.

I thank you, mothers of the disappeared. Through you, there disappears from my vocabulary, once and for all, the "problem of evil." To be replaced, thanks to your incalculable bravery, by the mystery of hope.

•

"I will disappear you." Grammatically as virulent and active as "I will murder you." The Spanish is vivid indeed, my first encounter with vivid grammar in any language!

They are disappeared from all but memory, that intractable power. This, although (according to the logic of Mack the Knife) "to be disappeared" is in fact a command, issued to poets or liturgists or dancers or singers—to any and all who remember. It is to-be-commanded-to-cease-to-exist. An instance, among other things, of radical materialism. Murder, that is, not only contemptuously denies personal immortality (in any case, who cares? since the deceased was troublesome or politically interfering or raised questions or conducted catechism sessions or was observed in the wrong places or knew so and so or reportedly said such and such . . .). Worse: the materialism, corrosive and cynical, would wipe out memory itself. The memory of the dead, lodged in the survivors. A message is transmitted to the living—forget them. To remember is mortally dangerous.

The mothers have refused this zone of silence, treacherous and inhuman as it is. They have broken through the cordon of terror. They march to the Presidential Palace, the U.S. Embassy, the Ministry of Justice. Year after year they vigil at the gates, as the limousines and Cherokees stream out, bearing the mighty who bear the life and death decisions.

What does it mean to carry the memory of the tribe? Or, equally to the point, what does it mean to forget? Or, to become unpleasantly precise, What does it mean to belong to a culture of amnesia?

•

Another aspect of memory is illustrated by the Solentiname Community.

Memory is an awakening-of-many, a kind of potlatch of the spirit. Everyone tosses in something—insights, scintillae, memories, fables. The pot simmers, savorous odors arise, more than words are in the air. Images, hints, parables, seasonal and diurnal events, undergoings and overcomings, graces embodied, the texture of life itself, and the gospel comes to bear, as memory renews the gospel.

So awakened, so cherished and evoked, memory is a kind of rebirth of dignity. "We are human, " say the mothers, say the peasants, "in the measure of our refusal to forget."

It is also a summons to action. Rise, let the bent knees straighten. Drop the short hoe, that slavish tool, and the machete. These are a curse; they are tools of mental incapacity, cringing, blind forbearance. Take up the Bible, read; do this in memory of me. And then, follow through. Act upon what you have seen.

The mothers cannot be understood merely as "remembering the dead" in some conventional or traditional way, as is done here and there on All Souls' Day. Something entirely different: something of threat and judgment, something both vulnerable and implacable.

They are like a band of Eumenides, these diminutive daughters of the soil, these former chattels. Their vigils, their chants and prayers are a judgment upon the atrocious injustice wrought on the dead. Meek ones, they march to possess the land. Or they are the mourners to whom is promised, not comfort, but strength.

The law commands amnesia, lifelong, as a price of survival. The good citizens obey, and forget. "None of my business; I saw nothing; I won't testify; I keep my hands clean; I have children; I have married a wife; I have bought a farm. . . . Yes sir, no sir, as you please, sir. . . ." The mothers remember. They carry in hand photos of the dead. They walk and stand and pray and recite names. Therefore Salvador cannot entirely forget. Crime and consequence, twin banished specters, appear once more. A better order has gained its sponsors.

•

We raise a glass to the cheerful bearing of sisters and priests, most of them foreigners—a word that says nothing of the firm root they take, and quickly. Surely a new generation of missioners is being born (as at home I see constantly at Maryknoll). No more "papa state (or mamma church) knows best." No more pushing an ideology from the compound.

This "option for the poor" sums up the change—a change

wrought first of all by the poor. The choice leads the missioners into dark waters indeed. Where else is the faith so hotly contested that its confession places one in mortal danger?

•

It occurs to me that theology, in the measure in which it draws on the insights of mystics and martyrs, flourishes or no. This had never struck me at home, for reasons best not gone into. Nevertheless the mystics offer a great gift to theology. An invitation not merely to formulate, speculate—but to "come and see."

•

A meeting with Jon Sobrino, Jesuit, theologian of liberation. A Jon of two trades, at least; a new kind of professional. Which is to say, as he laid out at some length, theology in El Salvador, as well as in other Latin countries, is a discipline of consequence. It could by no means be understood, let alone practiced, as a discipline in a void. Rather, it is nourished, given form and direction, by the poor, the base communities (which these theologians had helped form in the first place, the rhythm of developments being circular).

He was paying an explicit tribute; it became the theme of much that followed, in other exchanges.

These learned Christians, theorists, weavers of the volatile biblical words and themes—these are first of all, simply listeners, and not merely to one another, to academics within or outside their borders. Listeners to the unlikely poor, who (presumably and contrary to all prior historical expectation) have the good news—firsthand and by heart. And are thereby empowered, like the women at the Easter tomb, to convey it to others.

We heard all this before, how one went to unlikely places and persons to receive an unlikely word. And it struck us again—this "choice for the poor" is a dangerous undertaking. Everyone identified as having made such enters into mortal combat. For according to an immemorial order of things, the poor did not exist in order to be consulted—about the faith or anything else. They were enslaved; they were campesinos; that was all. Let them begin to lift their eyes on a horizon that stretched further than immediate survival, let them begin to add two and two, let them dare the conclusion, they would pay up—and so would their instructors.

Someone had whispered the forbidden words: two plus two equals———. A bullet might cut off the answer; but the equation stood on the air; eventually another would calculate it; all hell would break loose.

That was the trouble; there was always someone, some survivor; the word got around, a code, a secret conclusion, computed maybe on fingers or toes or in grains of corn or seed potatoes. And then nothing would ever be the same.

Thus many grew literate, and many died in consequence. And the primitive hornbook of literacy was the Gospel. It was momentous and ironic at once. For the former instrument of enslavement had also been a gospel of sorts, spelled out in bishops' palaces by mutual exegesis of dictators and their ecclesiastical lackeys; a word to be received on one's knees, in gratitude. Slaves, be content with your slavery, which is God's will for you. Or, heaven comes afterward; it is worth a lifetime of hell, here and now. Or, be assured, God's will comes to you through the ten families and the second estate.

Contrary to all calculation, a momentous journey began, even in Salvador. Its symbol was dramatic: the Exodus from Egypt; liberation from ignorance, subhumanity, untimely death, squalid housing, no medicine, and little food. Exodus from the Kingdom of Necessity, from fatalism and infantilism. From the human, defined by the few, enjoyed and exploited by them against the slow-moving wielders of hoe and machete and flail, the clods bent in the fields, human cacti, the ones fated to be born and eventually buried in the frayed hammock of the eternally disenfranchised.

Such as these, teachers of the taught? Yes, saith the gospel. Sobrino thus indicated once more, if we needed to hear it (and we did), the upside-down hermeneutic first commended by Christ: "He set a little child in their midst, saying: of such is the kingdom of heaven."

Twenty years ago, I reflected, little of this vision penetrated the borders to the north. A kind of blithe post-Vatican spirit was in the air. That our theology was white, male, affluent, that it could claim meaning only within a strict caste of color and class, that moreover it was offered in the midst of atrocious injustices—of this its practitioners were, for the most part, unaware. That little of real import could be offered until black theology and Latin theology and women's theology and Asian theology—at least these—had been heard from: of this we were, blissfully or otherwise, unaware.

And yet (I speak of those years as they touched on our lives) a kind of floating unease was in the air and took hold. It grew to a suspicion that all was not well, for all the prognostications from domestic Sinai. There was more to the real world than was being granted. What indeed of That World Out There? What of civil rights, what of Vietnam, what also of bellicose cardinals and piffling moral theologians and their stale *casus conscientiae?*

Pollen in the air, some landed and took root. The blacks were undertaking their own exodus; Vietnam was hottening up. And where were we?

"We had best be somewhere," I said to Philip in 1964. "We had best say something, and that quickly, under penalty of saying nothing—and the consequence of *that.*" (There being, in either alternative, consequence of moment.)

So we too started our exodus: from the war-making state, the mother and matrix of war as business, war as recovery, war as usual (along with opposite numbers, hell bent across Eastern Europe, across Afghanistan, a swath of domination and death . . .). By hook and crook, through clumsy and right thought, we were granted our own version of a base community, our own (perhaps in using the term dignify our efforts too much, we have yet to formulate things well) theology of resistance.

It has been a matter largely of reading as you run. We have had little help, in matters that seem to us of life-and-death import. We have yet to hear, after some twenty years of trial-and-error resistance, a word from a (male) North American theologian—a word indicating that our work offers a Christian insight into the times. (Women theologians, on the contrary, have been helpful in measure, especially Rosemary Ruether and Dorothee Soelle.)

Does the situation amount to a mutual impoverishment? I think so.

•

The waters have churned up unaccountably. Today most of us, like it or not, have a sense of being out of our depth, out of sight of land; friends in jail, family in trouble.

And the sorry business of nonviolent resistance is largely considered a dead end, even a scandal—in the U.S. and abroad. The churches close their doors, the bishops waffle, the famous pastoral letter is honored in the breach. Without something known as orthopraxis, orthodoxy withers on the vine.

This sophisticated first world of ours?

It seems to me that we are the underdeveloped, the technological campesinos. This is a sense I carry into Central America, a sense reinforced in most chastening fashion, as I linger and wander.

•

On a remote side street, led by Gene's infallible nose, we entered a modest Lutheran church; green paint of faintly nauseous hue, straightback pews, linoleum floors. We were seeking out the pastor, Medardos Gómez. He was, Gene said, not to be missed among the resisters in Salvador; imprisoned and tortured, he refused to leave the country, returning instead to his flock, and awaiting what, by common report, would be almost certain death.

Nothing grand here, no evidence of a church rewarded or furbished by the likes of Somoza. No plenipotent baroque, no cassocks, surplices, antependia, gorgeous saints in wood and ocher. No power, no trappings, no echo even of former power. We were at the heart of stern reformation.

A voluble woman aide received us. She too had been in prison, and undergone its rigors. *Sicut pastor sic grex.* We walked the length of the little church, toward the chancel. Beyond, an office, scarcely larger than its incumbent.

Pastor Gómez welcomed us with dignified gravity. A large man, and subdued. The look of a prisoner in his eyes; a look of those throughout the world, forced into a darkness laid like a coffin cover upon the living. A look of endurance, of patience wrested from unspeakable nights and days. (In Hanoi, a young communist guide and translator said to me, in a rare moment of candor: "I know the Christians. I can point them out in a crowded street." I asked astonished, "How?" He confessed not to know. It was something of "another world," something "different from our faces. . . .")

But how do you talk with the tortured? What topic, tone, will not trivialize their great torment, its memories and ghosts? I felt a kind of shame and confusion, forbidding that I lightly inquire of those who have been there, and somehow returned, the typography of hell. . . .

I once spent an hour in an Irish pub with a young religious brother who had been tortured in Argentina, and finally released and expelled. There were marks of cigarette burns on his arms and wrists. One did not poke about in the shadows of such infamy; rather I was grateful for the small talk at which the brother, being Irish, was adept. Thus did we keep the hounds of hell at bay.

But the brother had had great advantages, not available in Salvador. He had had two years to bind his wounds, as well as the help of psychiatrists. He was also a member of a group of the once tortured. And perhaps most important of all, he had been separated from that monstrous regime, once and for all.

No such relief for Pastor Gómez. He had returned, so to speak, from his grave, against all laws of nature, presumably also against conventional good advice. He sat here, welcoming us, at the scene of his crime. Indeed, in his case a plumb line could be laid down, crossing his brows, from crime to punishment—to intentional repeated crime.

Was he not a fool? (Conventional wisdom, the voices heard in the dungeon of Thomas More and Dietrich Bonhoeffer and Franz Jagerstatter and Dean Hammer and Elizabeth McAlister and Vernon Rossman.) Have such as these no thought for their children, the families whom their stubborn austerities, their intransigent virtue, are imperiling? . . .

The family, the children! How seldom, I thought, do we test them (and ourselves) against the steel of adult decisions—decisions which, come folly or right judgment, are at least our own, and even perhaps, now and then, deserve the name Christian. I look in the face of Pastor Gómez, remembrance numbs me. A recognition scene once more. Christian faces: let the world beware them!

There is no great point, I thought, in elaborating psychological theories about such people as the pastor. He is explained neither as simpleton nor extremist nor masochist. Given his world, his government, given religious faith and secular coercion—he is simply a criminal. He is infected from birth; he has the double indemnity of genetics and circumstances. Does he not issue from a long line of malcontents and protesters, does not his congregation ratify every disobedient instinct that arises in him?

Let us attempt to define the pastor's crime; it bears uncommon interest for us also.

It is this: he dares lead the common life of Christians. He opens his Bible; he reads there certain instructions and commendations. And then he proceeds to act, in the breach as he is, to act in the manner in which Christians throughout history have acted. He breaks through the smog of pseudonormalcy; he speaks out against unjust laws; he objects to murder. And worse still, he invites others to do likewise.

No wonder he is in trouble! For he exhibits openly before the world those characteristics extolled in his tradition and defamed by the state: courage, imagination, tenacity, solidarity with others.

Such virtues, it goes without saying, are available from the "treasure hidden in the field" of this world.

The common life. A life being led, in Salvador and throughout the world, often in equally unpromising situations, by multitudes. Therefore to canonize the pastor only isolates him, even as it dispenses others from the same calling. He is "doing his job," in the inelegant phrase, with a Christian twist. And in consequence, and with iron inevitability, the world is proceeding to do its job, which consists in impeding, by whatever means, his pastoral work. Removal, torture, threats against life—all to be taken in account beforehand, all part of the job.

The monotone went on; he spoke, for the large part, not about himself at all, but about the work at hand, the difficulties, the consolation. He never once raised his voice, or showed large emotion. Let the government indulge itself—flamboyant manifestoes, glitter, and glare. He was something else, a Lutheran, a reformer. He and his flock were called, not, God help us, to reform those as irreformable as D'Aubuisson and his squads. They must simply stand where they stood.

Might that not be the only hope—for D'Aubuisson also, and his monstrous bullies? a mere sign? A sign that big government, the government that eats, lives, and excretes polity, the government of ringmasters and of jackals, this bloody circus and bloody bread—this, though it pretend to be all, was not all. Not by a long shot, or even a short one. He was there, after prison, with his flock, to say so. Indeed he had no need to say it; he was there.

And as long as he was there, and those of his flock who were in prison knew he was there—why, the government was not all! It was as simple as that, and as final.

Something over against. Pastor Gómez and his people were the church. An upstart church, a transplanted one, a church poor and assailed, denounced as a gringo stronghold, a mere import. And yet, and yet—the church, the humiliated remnant, ridiculous, powerless, irrelevant. . . .

For all sorts of reasons, including the sanctioned frenzies of Salvador, Pastor Gómez's story is exceptional only because he is a pastor, therefore, at least in measure, visible. But for that, he would of course be lost in a vast international "method," a maze whose entrance and exit are everywhere and nowhere. The politics of megadeath barely pass him by; the method tried and true against Armenians and Jews and Palestinians and how many others whose removal from the earth would purportedly improve the lot of all.

The pastor finished his story of prison, release, return. He might have been recounting an average day in a farm parish in Iowa; something of statistics, births, marriages, deaths in safe beds, of old age and tired hearts. He was a very connoisseur of understatement, the dispassion of the survivor whose world must, for sake of sanity, be presented as bound by fairly normal routine.

A question. Was there not an ecumenical advantage working in his favor in Salvador? Which is to say, did not his imprisonment and torture occasion a public response, as would befall a Catholic priest in like crisis? After all, priests had been imprisoned and even murdered; and their deaths were a cause of international uproar. . . . His answer was that, no, unhappily these events are not perceived in the same way. When a priest is imprisoned, you must understand that the culture is shaken. He is part of a vast and ancient communion. So the death of a priest, let alone an archbishop, is a blow struck at the heart of history and of self-understanding; even to the unchurched it is seen as a kind of insult. But we Lutherans exist in a corner, out of the public gaze. We are not part of the culture, the history. Consequently we can be dealt with quite as they decide, and with impunity. . . .

When form is the object, the poet says, more is always less.

Pastor Gómez's words—the "less" of dispassion and gentleness and resolve; the "more" of suffering. I asked him if he would not pray with us, something from the Bible, the Beatitudes perhaps? He opened his testament and began, in Spanish. The same dry tonality, his pulpit tone, an all-purpose tone; of use, if not of distinction. A tone of exposition, counsel, mild reproof. It was a voice that could turn with his people to God in prayer; and beyond doubt had, for a lifetime. And whether in dungeons or courtrooms or interrogation centers or vans of death squads, I thought, this is the tone in which the church uttered its no; subdued, all but inaudible, but unshaken, unmistakable.

A voice of embodiment. You don't announce the Beatitudes as though they were a virtuous formula worthy of mere admiration. You embodied them; then your body was in your voice. As in the first instance, Jesus simply lived the blessings, before commending them to us. They flowered in spirit before they entered his flesh, in ways we know of. A right order of things. So simple, and yet how rare. . . .

We said our goodbyes.

But how does one say farewell to Lazarus, after the event, so to speak? We mumbled something, fell back on the old Christian premise and promise; when all else fails, pledge a prayer.

The remembrance of this man, his family, and his people floods back. He is someone recalled without recourse to a heroic image. A nondescript figure, anonymous in his rumpled suit, somewhat overweight (do the saints overeat, out of dread?). A shabby room, cheap religious oleographs on the wall, everything ordinary to the point of bathos. No methaphors, no myths; the human, in abundance and solidity, only that.

EL SALVADOR

When in prison, Bonhoeffer wrote, there is little to be done; tell the truth and say your prayers. Indeed.

(And I ask myself, Is there a great deal more to be done outside prison, given the times? and presuming that "telling the truth" is one with living the truth?)

•

Jon Sobrino again: the oligarchy are idolatrous, and the idols, as always, demand deaths. Perhaps idolatrous is too abstract; I mean to say, the oligarchy is itself a monstrous idol. You understand, to walk away from the idols, to refuse to pay blood tribute, is far more dangerous than to bow down. In the blasphemous temple where the wealthy worship, no age or sex or color is respected; all this grist for their jaws. But the preferred food of idols is children.

•

A relative of the disappeared fastened about my neck an infinitesimal cross of thread, woven by the political prisoners. I said, "It's like being inducted into the international fraternity of prisoners of conscience!" They were pleased at that, and managed a smile.

•

At the Jesuit provincial office, I noticed, as we came in, a machete on the wall, above a carven coat of arms of the order. Many of the disappeared have been found, hacked to pieces by machetes. And I wondered if *sua emenencia* understood how ambiguous a symbol his premises displayed?

•

The U.S. Embassy is a walled fortress of gargantuan height, breadth, and width, a hideous parody of Pauline cosmology, under one roof. Power stuck in concrete, the architecture of fear. It sets the mind aboggle, this astonishing seat of empire, set down amid its impoverished clients and vassals.

When form is unattainable, the poet implies, more is invariably less.

We found our way to the Department of Justice, seeking clearance to visit the political prisoners. An official spoke to us at length. His Spanish was, even to my primitive savvy, international-of-sorts. Which is to say, he was of that universal fraternity of bureaucrats who, here, there, and everywhere, dispense a largesse of delay, ambiguity, and shrugs, in worldwide offices of departments of purported justice. Somewhat like this: "The difficulties inherent in a project such as you envision, a project laudable in itself, is regrettably hedged about with all but insuperable difficulties. . . ."

He was loosening upon us blossoms of florid rhetoric; his eyes were alert as gimlets. "Alas, you understand, the clergy! Not all of them are aware of the necessity of keeping those politically suspect somewhat apart. Not from legitimate religious consolations [a quick bob of tribute] but from, shall we say, illegitimate expressions of solidarity. . . ."

With every bow of his vermicular body, every tic and wink and ploy, he was signaling the dumb gringos, if they could but read: Not a chance, boys. Get lost. Over my dead body.

His hair was dyed an unlikely crimson.

His talk reflected the feeble, earnest complexities of the disingenuous, lodged like embolisms in the arteries of power. . . .

This Office of the Redheaded League was awash with boredom and idleness. Justice, all said, being not only unattainable in the eyes of these secular millenarists, but, above all, to be opposed and dreaded.

Justice? Good Christ, who wants earthquakes, who prays for catastrophe? The women typed on, the desultory reports fell like smoke or darkness from their fingers. Etc. etc. etc. justice injustice just judges judgment. . . . . . . Hell is the geography of pure boredom, high noon in a government office consecrated to justice, which is to say, given over to the abuse of justice. The front office is paneled, air-conditioned; behind it languish those condemned to the stews of hell.

But hell is also out front; the jargon, the boredom. . . .

The only visible animation arose from this or that sotto voce conversation, behind the hand, into telephones. Work worth not a spit, clients lied to with straight face; nothing can be done, infinite regrets; the bored glances went past the discouraged shoulders of the helpless and victimized, the relatives following the trail of the bewitched and lost, a trail of bread crumbs through a wilderness. The trail ends here, the bread turns to stone.

It was Sobrino's sanctuary of idols once more.

There is momentary bustle and brisk trade; then there are slack hours, an off-season in hell. But more bodies will arrive by nightfall. This is the helicopter code, the Cherokee code, the napalm code. Only give us time, we'll deliver.

We waited and waited. Behind closed doors, officials consulted the auguries. But the planets were not in conjunction; we were turned away.

•

Everywhere the methods are alike. In jail you wait and wait: for an electronic door to open, for a guard to survey your pass, for a visit, for mail, for laundry, for food—for permission to exist.

At the Syracuse jail (the "Department of Public Safety") the prisoners' families wait in a bare corridor some six feet wide, sixty feet in length, without benches or chairs. Mothers and fathers, many of them infirm, wait sitting on the floor, for hours; they begin arriving at 6 A.M. in hopes that some three hours later they might be among the fifteen or so admitted to the cramped visitors' room. There the lucky ones, the early birds, are allowed at last to converse on inefficient phones, through plate glass, without ever touching or embracing, for one exact hour. Then, look sharp, time's up!

Justice delayed is injustice. Justice is invariably and everywhere delayed, but who names the local horror for what it is?

We are asked in a myriad ways to grow used to injustice; or, worse, to call it justice. Thus, in Salvador and passim: "The Department of Justice."

•

An extended conversation with Padre Pedras, S.J., director of the extensive, modern printing press of the university. He began with a kind of confessional statement, remarkable for its dignity and candor. How at the time of the Bay of Pigs fiasco he wholeheartedly supported the U.S. How that feeling of "anticommunism at any price" persisted in his life. Then, a second event served to reverse his thinking—a whirlwind of the soul, the invasion of Grenada. So that at present, in view of a probable invasion of Nicaragua, he would stand with the resistance.

It occurred to me while he talked that we three visitors had played the listener repeatedly, constantly, for some days now. When Pedras finished, I suggested that we had a story too; perhaps it was worth the telling. How four of my brothers had served in World War II. That in our family, as we grew up, it was understood that church and state were complementary entities, governed by mutual interests—never in the wildest stretch of the imaginable destined to be in conflict; each bespeaking, within its realm, the will of God.

That Philip suffered the cruelest and most complete change of all; from decorated officer in the European front of the war to priest in prison some twenty years later. That he was the first priest, to our knowledge, to be jailed for political resistance in America.

That for the past twenty years, in jail and out, we and our friends and families had kept something of nonviolence and resistance alive; not, to be sure, alive and well; merely alive. Not much indeed, but given the fact that by and large such actions as ours were rare indeed—something.

•

> Symbolic acts are gestures
>   made by Christian communities or individuals.
> Such acts do not always offer
>   definite or permanent solutions
>   to a problem of injustice.
> Still, because of their dramatic quality
>   they call public attention to the problem.
> Like prophetic witness, these acts
>   are sometimes quite effective
>   in fighting injustice.
>
> Pedro Arrupe, S.J.

•

The response of Pedras was courteous and subdued, a thank you amid silence.

This was the first time I ventured into autobiographical shallow (or deeps) in the course of this voyage. An ounce of boldness. . . ?

•

How can we know, in any detail, either the direction or the outcome of even our least valiant actions? We cannot. (I almost added, "in the nature of things.") I note the distress of spirit, the clearing of throats, and the shifting of feet that inevitably accompany the news that Elizabeth McAlister, mother of three, has chosen prison for her conscientious lot.

Nuclear resistance? All well and good.

"But what of the children?" is the cry, spoken, or caught short of speech. Dismay, terror of the unknown.

And something more than the "unknown" of prison. The equally and ironically unknown terrain of community. Elizabeth's children have lived in community since birth; they show, today, spontaneous trust in any of the several adults in the house. They can also be told, without risk of terrorizing them, of hard days to come, jail looming over parents and friends, separation, loneliness, prison visits (perhaps the most wrenching thing of all). Elizabeth writes of the first such visit:

> The umbilical cord is very strong. That of course reasserted itself this week, when the whole clan arrived. It was a joyful day, the fastest six hours of our lives. The kids were great, each making light of burdens, many hugs. But it had to end; and Katy (three years) is still learning about time and endings.
>
> "You'll come home with us, mommy?" She made it a question or plea.
>
> "No, but will you come back and see me again?"
>
> "Yes. But why can't you come home with us?"
>
> "Katy, I'd love to, but this is what jail is about. It will be awhile yet. . . ."

This is just too much reality for me! I understand it, but I don't like it! . . . The kids' letters are a joy. Being apart from them is the agony and burden and punishment. . . .

It is as though we were born disabled. Blind like the man in the gospel, we see others only dimly; they appear to the eye "like trees, walking." In such condition we make do. . . .
And then, and then an event, a breakthrough—healing.
It need not mean that illness or disability is relieved out of the blue. In most instances, something simpler but no less wondrous—new light is shed on an old impasse; that others have turned to us in compassion; our despair and alienation are not beyond the healing hand of friendship. "You are limbs one of another," Paul writes. More, "You are the Body of Christ, and member for member." Thus are offered ancient mystical resonances, which we once reserved for liturgies, meditation, homilies, a world of inner comfort and tentative worship. And hardly a thought given to the shrewd auguries being offered us, the political and psychological healing lurking in our scriptures.

Body of Christ indeed, and member for member! In another episode it is insisted by the Lord: the children enter first, into the arms of an Adult who, not of their blood line, forms about them the beloved enclosure whom we name Spirit.

•

TO ELIZABETH IN PRISON

Like a north star and its child
you shine there
among the wandering and lost
the stupefied, the victimized.

O my dear, there is gravity
and there is grace, and you
like a Vermeer woman
holding aloft a scales,
her face flooded with light
(the window open to pure day)—
must weigh, be not
found wanting.

•

The Lord speaks, in his own regard, of the *kairos,* a moment, an "after," both decisive and grace filled, a choice and a being chosen.

I think of myself, before Central America and after. No mere matter of putting one foot ahead of another, of a today which is no more than an enlarged or diminished version of yesterday. But a line crossed, a decision made. A *kairos* has been granted, something that appeared, on the face of it, quite neutral or unpromising or simply unknown—suddenly one is seized; a choice is demanded. . . .

Adults speak in somewhat this way of their baptism. Chesterton compares the moment of being flipped upside down in the world, then strangely set right once more, only to find that the formerly "normal" world, his world, is now itself upside down, out of kilter with his new insights, values, loves.

Dorothee Soelle writes of her "before" and "after." A child in Hitler's Germany, unconscious of the gathering terror, which in any case was leaving her untouched; and then the horror and revulsion that awakened her, from the eyes of a Jewish friend. . . .

Vietnam was, for many of us, a line drawn in earth and time. The "before" was the entire weight of our prior lives, the numbness of spirit with which we turned to the question of violence, the cultural and religious suppositions that left us infants in a dark wood. Then we crossed over—afoot or crawling, hesitant, dragging a great weight of the past. . . . And from thenceforth, life in America, in the church, in our families (in the Jesuits), could never be as it was. We had undergone a sea change; we were, for better or worse, new creatures.

These were deep waters, a very ocean of genesis. I am helpless to describe what transpired there, helpless as one who is himself the subject of change—changing, being changed, both dancer and dance.

One word in regard to the "after" comes to mind: freedom, that abused word. Something like this: in crossing a line (going to Catonsville, going to King of Prussia, to trial and prison), I threw off shackles, I breathed free. I felt no longer required to prove anything, as a condition for existing. Competition, achievement, goals, efficiency—let them go. I am summoned forth from the kingdom of necessity.

•

I hope I am not stretching the analogy to the breaking point when I reflect on the peasants and ourselves, and the common passage.

Dom Helder Camara speaks of the unlettered campesino as a kind of cactus, a prehuman. I know what he means, and not merely in Brazil. I bring his image home to myself, in America: insularity, force-fed innocence, racism, sexism, appetite, the assault of deceptive and disorienting media.

But for the gift of Christ, we are stuck in an interminable "before." Our only future is our past; which is to say, absolute moral stasis. We are stuck where we are. And our "after," if it be granted us, is as shocking a transformation, as though a cactus had stood on two feet and declared itself human.

We are bleached bones in a desert; then the bones stand, ankle to shin to thigh, and—but we know the rest.

•

To speak of crossing a line, being granted an "after." In 1980, a group of us, in violation of law, entered a nuclear weapons factory, a kind of latter-day Auschwitz-in-preparation. There we were able to effect a certain limited and symbolic damage against instruments of mass murder. Thus did we cross a line.

•

> We found a nuclear nose cone
> and in accord with the prophet Isaiah
> began its conversion
> "beating it into a plowshare."
> After pouring our own blood over it
> and over blueprints and desks
> we thanked the Lord's Spirit
> for guidance and protection
> and sang the Lord's Prayer.
>
> Philip Berrigan

EL SALVADOR

•

Without unduly straining matters, it seems to me that the campesino, like ourselves, chooses (or does not choose) to cross a line.

The law draws lines. The law reflects the culture, which is, here and to the south of us, a culture of rigid limits, whether one seeks access to property or class, or simply, as in the case of "classified" secrets, access to information.

The line is drawn by a machete in the hands of an oligarch across the dust of El Salvador. In the U.S. the line is drawn by a nuclear sword—at the gate of forbidden secret properties, nuclear arms factories, naval and air bases, research laboratories. The message is similar, overt or implicit: keep out; thou shalt not enter; lethal force in effect; enter under risk of death.

Many have died in Central America, for daring to cross.

What is less known, nearly the best kept secret of all, is how many have died in North America for daring to cross. (Sister Rosalie Bertel, radiation biologist, testified at one trial of nuclear resisters that some ten million nuclear victims have been created since Hiroshima, from the mining of plutonium and from the processing and deployment of nuclear weapons.)

•

Harsh times tend to clarify issues. They urge us closer to the bones of the gospel (those prophetic bones!). Thus certain commands, blessings, images of the Lord, once dismissed as "merely mystical" (which is to say, as romantic or irrelevant or to be verified only in the bye and bye)—these are shown for what they were meant to be: politically and humanly hot.

•

On the other hand. How easily so-called normal times (will someone please define these, the "normalcy" normally being in the eye of the possessor)—how often the times metastasize the good into the lesser good, or the lesser evil, roughly the same thing.

•

The mind permanently set aboggle; the extraordinary or extravagant or heroic—matter of daily occurrence. In such a world, such a time, it seems as though the truth can hardly be conveyed, short of hyperbole. Let me once more risk the latter, hoping to touch on the former. (And if hyperbole be my offense, I insist I am aided and abetted in that direction by all sorts and conditions of people: theologians, pastors, nuns, nurses, media reporters—coconspirators in a word.)

The theme is a kind of overvaulting of the truth, landing one on the other side so to speak; but having viewed things, meantime, in the round. A theme that runs through all discussion, that colors the politics, certainly, but runs deeper. It is a matter of steadfastness, standing by and with others; but more. Commonly, it comes through a story, a story to be lived out, first of all, then recounted to others (if one is lucky, and a good listener, one may hear it)—one to one; or more formally—to those at home, for example, as in the case of foreign missioners and professionals. These latter being a unique resource of truth otherwise neglected and distorted by media in their home countries.

Here is the theme, as I understand it, so utterly moving, so simple in the telling. It is the immense commonly acknowledged gift offered by the poor, the campesinos, the displaced; yes, and the ghosts of the murdered and disappeared—the gift offered to the favored or educated or skilled or traveled or whomever. To ourselves. The gift, once accepted, becomes something like a debt. Can the debt be amortized or canceled? If not, in what coin is it to be paid? One finds it being paid on all sides here: in the quality of the lives of these Europeans and North Americans, the risk and privations they undergo as a noble matter of course. Without them, the lives of the poor and victimized would be even more bleak, far less hopeful, than they presently are. . . .

Harsh times and their ironic gift.

Who could have predicted, forty years ago, that the Sermon on the Mount, with its improbable blessings conferred on unlikely people, that such words, blessings, commendations, would become (what they were all the time, only we were blind) our sole hope in the nuclear glare and shadow?

Love your enemies? For centuries we concluded fondly that such words were to be taken with a grain of salt. They were the words of the Holy One, granted; but they were uttered for the sake of the saints, not ourselves. They had nothing to do, no light to cast, on the violent give and take, the hurly-burly of secular life. Precious little light, moreover, to offer "moral beings in immoral society."

So we made our so-called choices: love or hate, crusades, pogroms, auto-da-fé; inquisitors on the one hand, Francis of Assisi on the other; bullets or bread, a casuistry of allowable murder.

By such a torturous route we came to our own lifetime, to Hiroshima. Only now, as we dimly realize, does the scope and force of that irrelevant Sermon on the Mount dawn on our benighted conscience.

Love your enemies: a command of such immediate import, so crucial, it hurts where we live, hurts as we die; or prepare to.

Indeed, nukes, in a malign artistry far beyond the crass knowhow of their creators, have narrowed the human choices. We will develop structures, methods—dare one say, a spirituality—of nonviolence. Or we will perish.

•

I pray for others. In face of a suffering I can never hope to understand, much less have part in. Perhaps it is a mercy, this numbness. Perhaps the more I try to understand, the more I miss the mark. Who indeed could hope to grasp this tortured land, the evil let loose on it?

Stand under it, let the wave pass over. A conversion, preparation.

•

A phone call reports that the trial in Syracuse, a long state of siege, is going into a fourth week. How I long to be there with Liz, Phil, friends, the children! Yet to be here with the Mothers of the

Disappeared, in the camps, among the displaced—this must be my all too literal translation of being on trial at home.

•

We end each day with a discussion of the events, places, people encountered. One night the subject came up—Christians and worldy systems of justice. The occasion was the recent trial of the soldiers who murdered the religious women in 1980. I asked: Have the relatives of the slain concluded that, with the soldiers convicted, justice has been done and the dead may rest in peace? And pursuing matters further, supposing the collusion of higher authority, would tracing the crime to its maniacal source solve anything? Did those sublime Christians, the murdered sisters, themselves believe that justice is to be achieved in this world? The brother of one of the martyrs, we were told, could not bring himself to attend the court or let his eyes rest on the killers. But if not he (I dared raise the question), then who is to forgive, reconcile, verify in deed the reconciling deed of Christ?

I thought there was evidence in our testament, in the letter of James, in Paul's letters—and most of all in the treatment of Jesus at the hands of systems of justice—evidence for the following: that forgiveness, to the point of absurdity, is our response to injustice; and that the early church regarded civil and criminal courts as off bounds, along with the military, to Christians (always excepting, of course, their being dragged into court as defendants, invariably for "healing in that Name" [Acts, 4]).

I recalled, in this regard, the tragedy of a young Catholic Worker, murdered wantonly on a New York street, within a year of his wedding. His new widow summoned me on an urgent request: Would I visit the men charged and jailed for the killing? and, further, would I assure them that she forgave them? And insistently: Would I inform the police authorities that under no circumstances would she appear at trial as witness for the prosecution?

And recalled the example of my friend the Buddhist monk, Thich Nhat Hanh. A number of his students had been murdered in Saigon during the latter stages of the war. The murderers might have been Viet Cong or Americans or soldiers of the Saigon regime; it was open season, from any and all sides, against those who refused to take sides, to take up arms. The Buddhists' response to the tragedy was prompt. In an advertisement published in a Saigon daily, they announced forgiveness of the murderers; and more: that they would refuse all cooperation with any "justice inquiry. . . ."

Then Dennis recounted a recent close call. He had been mugged on a Washington street shortly before our departure from the country. A knife was held to his throat, as he handed over his wordly goods. Forgiveness? He confessed to confusion and anger. . . .

I recalled that James' letter to the church excoriates Christians who in spirit align themselves with the rich, the rich who in turn "oppress you, . . . who drag you into courts, . . . " who thereby "blaspheme that honorable name by which you are called."

In her one-to-one insistence on loving service, Dorothy Day seemed closer to these views, we thought; and let it go at that.

•

We hear again and again from base communities, theologians, students, missioners: El Salvador is a church of martyrs. It seems to me that we have not the slightest inkling of what this means. But I wonder if the church of martyrs has affected the Jesuits, and if so, how.

Certainly something new is in the air. It is not merely that the university undertakes quality research in so many areas—research that brings a measure of sense into the incoherent situation. Or that the university itself survives against such odds.

I mark as more important than all this, the Jesuits' solidarity with the victims. And, in consequence, a theology whose metaphors and insights and themes are neither arbitrary nor thoughtless nor abstract.

All this and conviviality too. Jesuits who can sing in the furnace of tribulation.

•

Base communities. Everywhere I venture I hear of them: America North and South, Western and Eastern Europe. They cross all sorts of political and cultural barriers, springing up everywhere like miraculous blossoms.

They seem to me, in fact, to offer a basis for any future worth considering. And I mean this not only in regard to the church. They are also an important clue, a human order in the midst of stalemated and brutal social arrangements.

I note too that for two decades we have been developing our own form of such communities. Civil rights days, Vietnam, the years of the nuke—all have urged the essentials on us: biblical alertness and literacy, political responsibility. This is the life we have been leading, with a hectic eye on the public storm. Jonah House, Catholic Worker, Sojourners, Kairos, POTS, Emmaus House, Ailanthus, so many others. Places where we could stand together, points of geography we could move from and return to. Where common symbols, commonly understood, rendered destructive conflict null and void.

•

Questions of moment for Jesuits, questions that touch our lives everywhere: Are we capable of something better than go-getting and going it alone? short, that is, of the desperate conditions that create the "something" in El Salvador?

Children of a cutthroat culture, we drag along with us into the order a weighty baggage of competition, irascibility, spunk. No wonder then that we end up coffined like armadillos in our attainments, specialties. And if truth were told, lonely as only those can be who are called to something other than "honors . . . the credit of a great name. . . ."

•

A night ago I dreamed this: I was wandering through a field, free and witless as a pheasant—and just as hungry. And wandered into a patch of wild strawberries.

Had the dream proceeded for another minute or so, dislocating and delicious as it was, I swear I would have awakened with the stain of berries on my mouth, so vivid was their taste. . . .

Is this a reversion to childhood and our big berry patches, where the pheasants looted us each autumn, honking in derision, running through the fields like jack rabbits, then mounting in air with a great whirr and blur, as we chased fruitlessly after?

•

The Syracuse trial haunts me as we journey southward. Emblem, enigma? Who is to say which?

When I speak of the trial and mention that a member of my family is once more on the block (and certain to be convicted and jailed), there is an immediate alleluia! It is as though a sten gun had been pushed aside by an intervening hand. Which indeed it has.

•

Another dream. I was flying in a small plane that rose to a hundred feet or so, wobbly as a kite in a gale, and thereupon began to cough and falter in alarming fashion.

Then instead of obeying the fearsome law of nature and ruinously spiraling downward, my diminutive bird floated down like a very feather—on a rooftop as it chanced. And there disgorged us all, alive and shaken and none the worse. A dreamlike version of life above reconciled with life below, a consonance of welcome and deliverance.

Now I thought this was a marked improvement over the crash script of my normal New York disaster dream, in the course of which everyone aboard, including the dreamer, invariably is blasted earthward from some improbable height.

Maybe here, salvation is less unlikely than at home?

•

Yesterday Jim Harney came in unexpectedly, a very apparition on the threshold. An unlikely meeting! An old friend from Boston who did time during the Vietnam War as an honored member of the Milwaukee Fourteen. Shrewd, an Irishman of soul and substance, older now (a common threnody, I sing it of him, he of me). A kind of transcontinental commuter, north and south; he often disappears for weeks in the mountains here, where he lives with the endangered people, takes miraculous photos and gathers information on bombings, disappearances, the fate of the forgotten. Then back to the States; he travels coast to coast, telling his stories. A weaver of history, but his best story never gets told, his own life. I saluted him in wine, the old man of the mountain, and he laughed from his deep cavern of a face.

•

We question one Jesuit or another as to his field of competence. Varied indeed, as would be the case wherever they hung out a shingle: sociology, economics, media, theology. What is remarkable is that the discussions invariably come around to a few basics: the plight of people, the martyred friends, the displaced, the war, Reagan, the ominous future. It's as though a percussion sounded somewhere on the horizon, in the ravines, the pitiless clay fields, the embattled volcanos where soldiers battle to a bloody draw; as though a sonic boom of destiny sounded, and were synchronized with the heartbeat of scholars and priests. One immense tormented body—and themselves to give it voice. And they invariably add: since the persecution started, we've drawn closer to one another. Persecution is the clue, the bloodshot clue.

•

A word of tribute to Gene, our dauntless mentor, guide, translator. Gifted with a kind of second sight of mind; I swear he sees around the ninety-degree corners of life and its wrongs and wrys.

Quite literally, North American born and bred, he knows everyone and everything knowable about Salvador. Try him. Does he confess now and then ignorance of some fact, unacquaintance with someone? If so, you may safely strike them from your list.

Gene lives close to the bone, the bone of prayer and poverty; a Giacometti world of which he is an admirable emblem. Told me in passing, when questioned, that he would not undertake to teach courses at the university here since his Spanish is (here a puckered brow and a pause) only, say 95 percent perfect, not one hundred.

A mind honed to an edge; better, a mind all edge.

I wish that many others than ourselves, those discouraged or at wits' end or simply stuck in the U.S., could know that such as Gene exist—out of the big glare and blare, the venomous blaze of media.

EL SALVADOR

He pitches his tent in a convent of delightful nuns. He is regarded there as a kind of Gabriel the annunciator; good news in a bad time. And earns what might loosely be termed a living, sending dispatches of news to New York radio stations, Associated Press, as these entities may, at times random and rare, grant him access to their magic—for a moment of truth. Thus the truth, like himself, ekes out an existence of sorts in the naughty world.

•

Laid low, north and south, with a "case" of what I privately refer to as organic exopathy. Nothing like an opaque polysyllabic and to cover a dread disease!

Laid low, lower by far than sea level. A raving case, all sluices open. Getting rid of the U.S.?

Alas, a morning of travail follows on a night of same; and I, landlocked, unable to accompany my pith-helmeted compañeros as they venture into parlous parts. Solitary I keep the cat who keeps the house; I ornament this journal, a shaky hand and brain. . . .

The mystery intrigues; every viand I partook of, the others did also. Yet they thrive, while I buckle under. How come? Can it be I have more of dregs, dodges, and damnations to be ridden of?

Mockheroically, the thought of demise intrudes. What a gas, exclaimed Gene, if Berrigan were to perish in Salvador of emetic rot!

I was hardly amused, and stared him down, putting a good if pallid face on things. Yet to this papery confessional, I confess: the prospect, even remote, was daunting. Everybody wanta go to heaven (sing it out) but nobody wanta die!

•

The days are crowded with recognition scenes; a sense that I've been here, there, before. I walked these barrios, these dusty sun-drenched streets, years ago. . . . Summarily ordered out of New York during the war in Vietnam—those bizarre maniacal five months! Latin America, up horizon and down dale, volcano, glacier, from head to tip of a continent I wandered. Last night, I listened as Harney, uncorked at last, let loose his vapors, pouring a stream of reminiscences of his years in Salvador, saying things I seem—vicariously, intimately—to have known for years (and yet could not have known, except from that other side that tips toward one in sleep)—the bombing of volcanoes, the drone of copters, the tunnels crowded with terrified peasants riding out the bombardments. . . . Nightmares I sweated out in Hanoi in 1968; the days and nights that led me, as though by the burning path of an arrow, to Catonsville and crime.

To what will these days lead? The question is presumptuous and unanswerable—like Job's.

•

A kind of preternatural clarity descends after illness. As though the guts, freed of their onerous task, were one with mind at last, one vivid peristalsis.

I think of those I love, the friends on trial, Carol in Italy, Jerry and family, Phil and the children, others far and wide. And I take heart. Free of *mal du pays,* free of the absurdity of my gypsy existence. This is my litany of hope: the church of the victims, the Eucharist of the poor, the cloud of witnesses here enlarged, the fiery lightning of Christ the martyr. Christ humiliated no more, knifed, shot no more, drawn and quartered no more. Death no more, in the land of death multiplied, death the torrid, death the toreador.

Squalid death, devised by squalid minds. "The terrible thing is," someone said mournfully to us, "they not only torture and rape; but they throw the bodies in garbage heaps and dumps. It is in such places we must search for those we love."

•

Purification, the *via purgativa.* You come here, you assure your soul you have other intentions than those of tourists or newshawks. Then someone or something retorts: That's your story!

And it starts. And the longer you stay, and the more truly you pursue that "other way," the more terribly it takes hold.

It matters altogether where one chooses to pitch a tent; on the embassy lawn or in the camp of the displaced. There is an option for the poor, and an option of the damned.

•

In which regard, I think of Merton. The half of his soul, at least, was Latin. This was the poet half of him, the ungovernable part, his affliction and glory. It was the part that made for friendship; a friendship that, in our case, goes beyond death itself. How naturally my thoughts turn to him, as this trek proceeds! In the early sixties, he unrolled one of his scenarios (one among how many, this one wholly Latin in its flamboyant logic). He would go to Latin America with two or three companions; the first volunteers being a monk psychiatrist and a monk saxophonist. Somewhere on the edge of some city they would set up a kind of house—house of prayer, house of access, house of music (and given the trio, as I thought, a house of much more).

There were, however, other givens; call them the times and the authorities. Given these, the plan was pure fantasy. Either Merton didn't understand this (he was congenitally incapable of grasping the Byzantine character of politics, in church or state) or, knowing it, didn't care.

Such midsummer nights' dreams, airy and inventive and responsible as they tried to be, they were offered to keep others going as well as himself. They were a kind of poetry of the oppressed. And who was not in need of a poem or two, stuffed in a bottle, tossed in the sea, landing God knew where?

Speaking of poems and poets. At Cornell in 1968 a group of us were picnicking by a stream. Someone suggested we read our verses aloud. Then one of the students fashioned a page of poetry into a paper boat and floated it downstream. There went the poem, for good.

And that was the way with Merton. In fragile ways his hopes were launched, given away utterly into time's current. They are still coming ashore.

•

My journal is like those boats too; jaunty, unseaworthy, absurd. But in Salvador, poetry, and more, can be salvaged. As

I'm discovering. Among things dragged ashore, waterlogged, revived—the freedom to remember Merton as I knew him. Merton the friend. Not Merton the industry, the calendars chock-full of wise sayings, the memoirs at third or fourth remove, the sedulous peering at minutiae, the speculations and scandalmongering. The U.S. loves heroes; and makes sandwiches of them.

•

Occurs to me, as I see the harsh life Christians are forced to lead here, that in the U.S. we need a better culture—or a worse. Stalemated, bereft as we are there, we do what we can, creating small circles of sanity in which, at least now and then, we breathe free.

•

Downtown in San Salvador, we saw a lofty straw overhang, like an eave without a roof, wilting in the stew of sun and downpour. Only this relic is left of the platform and altar where the Pope celebrated Mass on his visit. That and the tall spire and cross above, just adjoining the colonial government buildings.

One priest said bitterly, "He came here and sang the Mass and preached; then he dined with the officials and departed. The mothers of the disappeared sought a meeting and received no answer. It was a renaissance pope's visit. And many of us wished he had stayed at home, where Opus Dei and his own banks' murky dealing should keep him occupied."

•

Keeping this diary, groping after something that lurks just the other side of things, half remembered. As though like a sleepwalker summoned by ghosts, I was granted entrance to places forbidden the living; and then, on return, commanded to forget what I had seen. I wonder, sitting here at the crossing of streets—workmen straightening a garden, children walking to school—have I been here before? Who were my leading angels? and what have I forgotten, and at what cost?

•

A torrid, cloudy day after an all-night storm, pyrotechnics of awesome dimension. A storm fit to bring on the last day. Then the usual day limped in, an excuse of a day—and this in the tropics, where dawn invariably blazes in, a baroque entrance, almost an outcry, at the sights dawn will reveal.

•

From anger free us, O Lord. But only from such anger as, in face of the injustice of things, leaves us literally at sea, rudderless.

This was the smoldering mood of the woman from the U.S. who visited here last night. The others who accompanied her, Mennonites, were contained and silent before her stormy outpouring. Something slowly clarified: they have lived here for several years, working and coping in the miserable camps, while she was newly arrived. Yet their even temper could by no means be interpreted as mere resignation. Rather, I thought, they had weighed things emotional, how to continue one's work without going literally berserk (decapitated corpses, the raped and tortured). They had not gone mad; they had come to a singleminded, dogged sanity.

•

Presupposing the existence of someone called God, and of some entity called the human soul—one asks what happens to those who commit such atrocities as occur daily in Salvador. This, it seems to me, is a more serious question than the fate of the victims. These at least have a promise; but the executioners, a judgment.

•

I read of the following. Two writers, one in a huff of vanity, the other in a puff of spleen, departed from their "investigative tour" here, and cut out for home.

The writers' cramp, stuck in ego.

•

Tourist or no, simpatico or no, good listener or no, one is assailed from time to time with both isolation and alienation. This is hell—with an exit visa. Or the mood shifts, the sun comes out; this is heaven on a three-week pass. Not being quite up to meriting either, I do my best, take what's offered and run with it. A hint of warning, a foretaste.

•

Our companion Dennis is a Jesuit on the move. No monad in the void he; he comes from somewhere, stands somewhere, moves toward something. He enjoys of course a great advantage, being an artist to start with—an advantage far beyond the merely esthetic or practical. It enables him to judge his powers, to reckon with accuracy the distance yet to be covered.

I speculate that he was born with a third eye (curse and blessing both); and in consequence, has no eye at all, right or left, for the main chance. I sense a quiet dynamite in his presence, a modesty altogether winning, a talent that has already reckoned its price.

I think, with something very like envy, of how lucky he is. He has yet to undergo the attrition of the years; he's unmutilated by sour memory. So I do well to take my cue from his innocence rather than my own disabling experience.

Being with him is a rare joy. We laugh and clown intemperately. In a way that demands denial of nothing in my life, he lends me new eyes to see with, a chance of forgiveness, starting over.

•

Day after day the vicious choppers rip at the sky, like the scissors of fate. They torment the earth's open wound, stitching, unstitching by turns.

The mercy mission of the merciless; the copters bring in the casualties from the battle areas to hospital. Then, as though to clarify priorities, they load up with phosphorous bombs and careen off, heading for the volcanoes and the guerrillas.

•

Returning from a nearby village with Jim Harney. Without ado, he asked the driver to pull over, said a brisk adieu, and was off.

This seems to be a specialty among the aficianados here, this melting into the crowds; maybe it's the urban version of the guerrillas, miles from here, appearing and then disappearing into the flora. Spectacular and modest and tactical at once.

•

Someone told us, a provocative word indeed, that it might be possible to tour the campus of the state university. All we needed! We set out in twilight, arrived at the fenced-in area, came on a gate and went in—relying, in case of emergency or challenge, on our capacity for blank looks, the gringo tourist mode.

What we were unprepared for was the scope of devastation. We knew—everyone knew—that in 1980 the army, provoked by the students, descended on the campus and cleaned out the nest of rebellion. But seeing is—more than believing; it is being struck numb. It was as though vandals had cut a swath across a civilized vista. We wandered about in a daze, never having witnessed, on any academic acre anywhere in the world, such lunar desolation. Does the spirit haunt those places where it once dwelt, especially those places it loved, those native to its powers? Burnt out, pillaged, gutted, so proud and beautiful a creation, brought so low.

Eventually, we were shadowed by two guards, armed with machetes. First we decided to ignore them (blank looks, tourists). Then another ploy; Gene turned about, engaged them in queries both suave and solicitous. Could it be that, all unknowing, we were in fact trespassing? If so, a thousand pardons, señors. We are not? A thousand thanks. And could you possibly enlighten us as to a rumor we have heard, to wit, that this great university, the proudest of all Central America, is shortly to be opened once more? We ask this, you understand, as North American scholars, with a special love of your country, your culture. . . .

By now, the machetes were nowhere to be seen, the formerly silent tongues grew voluble. Proud indeed were they of their university; its opening was not only probable, but imminent, we are pleased to inform you. Permit us if you please (this with a flourish of the snickersnees, now transformed into instruments of courtesy)—permit us to be your guides; the most presentable edifice of our alas stricken campus remains the School of Law.

So thence, and under such patronage! A cleanup of the building had made considerable progress; books were in place on shelves, study alcoves were cleaned and restored.

But the Department of Education was, alas, another matter. We wandered awe-struck among debris: classroom, laboratory, lecture hall. It was as though a torch had been set against the combustible soul of the place. A mockery of the mind; wreckage, ashes, rubbish. And on the walls in crimson paint, like a last cry of the doomed, the incendiary slogans. It was as though a dying shout were stopped by an arrow in the throat.

What does it portend, this absolute hate of the human, of its capacity and noble task—so to hate that in the countryside, violated bodies lie; and in the capital, the pride of a tradition is brought low?

They had dragged the medical equipment from the building, burnt it, wrecked it, sold it in the streets.

The empty sockets of windows, and the blackened evidence of fire within.

Indistinguishable heaps of books, leaflets, emptied file cabinets.

Wild birds, crows, swallows, nesting, darting in and out of windows and doors, unimpeded; dung, filth. Abomination of desolation.

And yet we heard from the lips of two unlettered men, set to guard the tomb; *Our* university, it will open again.

•

Came a relief, and no mean one at that. An invitation to sup with a group of nuns of the Passionist order. It happens again and again, the common chord is struck in such communities; laughter, an unrancorous steadiness under pressure. (Those Christian faces again!)

In the inelegant phrase, the seven women had seen it all. On the score of losses they were, so to speak, front runners; such losses as welled in their eyes and made gentle mockery of their composure.

No (in answer to a query) no, we were not allowed, after the soldiers did their worst in our villages, not allowed to bury the dead.

We who had escaped were forbidden to return. They pushed our dead into a mass grave; and we could only pray at a distance for them, as best we might. We must leave them to God. (Who was to be so left, whether killers or victims, they did not specify.)

And the killers, the *escuadras de la muerte,* do they consider themselves Catholic? Are there priests and bishops who tolerate such outrages?

Regrettably yes. You must understand that at least two bishops denounced Archbishop Romero as "chief of all communists." Thus, as least indirectly, they supported the massacres.

Living with death; something akin to living for life's sake.

●

Fear comes and goes, no great trauma. Only a little twinge of mortality at the back of the mind.

●

We resolved early on to read a passage of scripture each evening, to be followed by silence, prayer, voicing of such needs as occur.

Alas for excellent intention! We come in exhausted, the mind starts its dance; events, people, places crowding in. . . .

And Romero's image is hung on every wall; it becomes a kind of afterimage on the retina. "He stands for us all," they say, always in present tense. No one is "disappeared" in this supersensibility of faith, the persistence of memory.

●

Like enormous road signs to utopia, the political banners stretch across streets downtown: "Duarte, President of Peace!" "VOTE ARENA [D'Aubisson's party] AND DEMOCRACY

COMES TO SALVADOR!" "DEMOCRACIA AHORA!"

And en route to the airport, a soldier, bigger than life, gun at ready, a billboard macho: I will give my life for my country!

Such confabulations are particularly ironic. Duarte is presently and uneasily in power; as indeed he was intermittently during the most savage time, 1980, when, among many others, Romero and the U.S. missioners died.

•

In New York, Dennis had agreed to undertake a mission of mercy on behalf of a Salvadoran family and their relatives. We were instructed to seek out the mother of the family in a village some distance out of San Salvador. Thereupon, our first adventure by bus.

The father, we learned, had been killed some months previous, and the mother, a strong-minded matriarch, was determined that the sons be airlifted out of like danger. So we embarked in a speedy land animal, churning its dust-ridden way through the countryside. At each stop, peddlers of every vittle under the tropical sun climbed aboard, musically, never once prosaically, calling their wares. There were fruit drinks in plastic envelopes tied about a plastic straw, great woven straw bowls and baskets of papaya, mango, oranges, bananas; and newsboys crying the latest purported (and certainly censored) national doings. Also strips of coconut and various sticky concoctions, at which Gene cast a rolling minatory eye. And so on and so on.

Finally, after an hour's progress through a landscape fit to try the mettle of the original Pilgrim, our dromedary drew up at a bustling village market. We dismounted, to be greeted by the mother and her youngest son, a hefty, handsome sixteen-year-old, anxious to test his Engleesh, at which study he had attained, he told us proudly, lezzon twelf.

We entered the single room of their home directly from the street; no windows, a great double (or triple or quadruple) bed at the corner; the other half of the room occupied by table and chairs, an abandoned refrigerator, an immense standing closet. And then, inordinate and unexpected, a very shrine of technology, a classy stereo and radio.

Dennis had brought along a tape recording from the son. We listened; the mother wept in her apron. Lengthy warnings to his brothers, protestations of well-being to his mother, instructions as to the journey to El Norte.

A dish of fresh pineapple was served; it was to prove my intestinal undoing, which got underway that midnight.

Mercy casts a veil over the sequel; some thirty-six hours of uncontrollable rumblings, off any known seismograph.

•

Then by plane to San Miguel and San Francisco Gotera and the Franciscans in the war zone.

We taxi to the airport, the sky buzzing feverishly with copters and military planes. War, rumor, fortunes of war. No assurance the flight will take off. Indeed, complications multiply; the bridge between Gotera airport and the town was blown up months ago; now, we learn, the temporary bridge is also *hors de combat,* under repair. So even if step one is accomplished by air, no one can guarantee we will reach our hosts, or they us. . . .

Shall we chance it, nonetheless? We put heads together, decide to take our chances, Buddhist fashion, one travail at a time. . . .

Over Lake Ilopango we wing it, a stunning steel-grey sky, the verdant land teeming with life, teeming with death. Helicopters weave and veer, slaphappy, insects of war, "scorpions with stings in their tails." In and out of thunderheads, we see, as the copters snoop about, the military, drab uniforms through the open doors. . . .

Six hours later, *mirabile*! We sit among the missioners, on their airy porch in Gotera; it is surely one of the loveliest, most humane episodes of our stay.

But first to the saga of the bridge.

We landed; no airport building as such, only a few haphazard shacks scattered about, gaseous juices and suspicious confections for sale. News was again bad: the bridge over the San Miguel River (which is to say the hypothetical bridge, the real one long since blown up by guerrillas) was damaged by heavy rains. So we started out, a point of no return (and barring unusual luck, a point of no continuance). Picked up by a passing truck. And so arrived at said hypothetical bridge; thus far and no further.

As to the original bridge, its central span hovered in midair, like a gigantic abandoned mass of spaghetti; strands, cables, struts; in a fit of revolutionary fervor they were tossed to the sixteen winds.

Gene offered: let me see what's occurring at the other end of all this. And on foot, in despite of all gravity and good sense, undertook the dizzying roller coaster progress, along the tortured metal frame. Thus was he last seen, for hours.

A rumor went the rounds; take hope; an alternative to the defunct alternate, lying some four or five kilometers to the east, will shortly be opened.

Meantime there is a wait to be endured, say until (a grandiose wave of arms) 4 or 5 P.M., when the span, and the road appertaining thereunto, should be rendered once more passable.

So we hung our metaphoric harps on the willows by the waters of desolation, under the merciless Salvadoran sun. And were, in the long meantime, entertained by sundry unquenchable small fry, against whom we tested our faltering Spanish, and they their ditto English.

And at length, another Samaritan truck. We proceeded, our progress comparable only to an ancient serial disaster film in which "The Perils of. . ." are finally and triumphantly surpassed and our heroes arrive toward sunset at the seat of fame and fortune and are greeted by. . . . We discovered our lost Gene, who had meantime discovered our patient Franciscan host, Jerry.

And so made our final stage, triumphant and chastened at once, in driving rain. And so arrived at the mission.

As we turned into the gate of the compound, we had our first glimpse of the military. A huddle of khaki, mere striplings, taking shelter in the area. How pitiful they appeared, pinched and cold, wet to the pelt, these young forced draftees, heads shaven, thrust into ill-fitting uniforms.

We could see in their faces wonder, bewilderment; and from the missioners, a cool verging on coldness. The climate held steady, a temperate endurance. "We survive only because the American Embassy sent the word out to the military: cool things; no more priest killings," Jerry said wryly. A thin lifeline indeed, a chancy word of power.

A good solid Irish supper. Afterward, beer and spirits on the airy porches. We were joined by two Mennonite nurses and a nun from the U.S. Conversation got underway. I had the impression, here as elsewhere, of extreme reticence regarding the touchy question of violence. The hottest subject of hot times, by far. Could the explanation lie in the fact that everyone, like it or not, Christian or no, priest or no, the peaceable and the incendiary—everyone was drawn into the firestorm?

I think I understood. We three were witnessing a complicity of sympathy, in the most basic sense. An understanding, on the part of the noble men and women, that the church must stand by the victims, assuaging, counseling, forgiving, interceding; a holy backup of an unholy war.

Every one of them regretting the war, everyone part of the war. A war that, like a grass fire spreading to underbrush, spreading thence to a tinder forest, was scattering lives hither and yon, a furious scramble for survival. Some ditching the blaze, some discernible in the smoke and glare, feeding the flames. But the blaze, the one event! Everyone drawn to it, everyone suffering its cicatrices of body and soul.

Everyone talks about the war; but the war is like the weather, a fact of nature, beyond control. Hardly anyone ventures, "We can do this or that to mitigate the war." Off bounds, evidently, by common agreement; the part we play in the war. And even more touchy, a plain statement of opposition to, aversion toward, any and all war. I knew the subject was the heart of the matter; and yet I was stymied. Thinking of the analogy of the body, that the heart can rarely, if at all, be uncovered, and then with mortal peril.

And yet. There were circumstances when it was imperative to uncover the heart. If the heart (as in that heart of the matter called war) was diseased and the disease had become a very epidemic.

Only surgery would help; the surgery we name candor, leveling with one another. (Each of us being, undoubtedly, the patient.)

We three voyagers, along with those on trial and in prison at home, had staked something on such premises as these; better surgery, even the most dangerous and radical, than terminal disease.

Staked—something? By Salvadoran standards, which are those of the heroically murdered and endangered, not a great, deal, as simple eyesight would reveal by horrid contrast. But still, something.

It was in virtue of that something that we were received everywhere with such courtesy and warmth. Even while, in practically every instance, a kind of dance of distancing got underway. All moved in unison, there was give and take and sparring and feinting—but the rules forbade touch.

That night, initiated by the two nurses, the subject was broached at last. It was my impression that on the instant, a halt occurred in breathing: relief, dread, listening.

I was obviously being thrust on stage, the notorious one of the three. What did I think of events in Salvador? How would I respond to the provocation thrust at young campesinos and students and, yes, priests and nuns; after the fifty thousand murdered and disappeared; after stalemate of church and state around self-interest, property, and power; after the years of casual murder-as-usual? (They were questions that made me wish with all my lily-livered soul that I had stayed in my own backyard, cultivating those *fioretti* commended to us as the blooms proper to monks. . . . Except that at home, too, the same questions arise, vigorous weeds among the flowers.) Might as well take the plunge:

—It was one thing, I suggested, to agree that violent self-defense was itself defensible. It was quite another to bless, baptize, confirm, or otherwise anoint or sacramentalize the conclusion. I could discover, after years of search and study, no evidence that Jesus, in word or deed, condoned violence, whether socialized and indeed canonized in war, or up close, tooth against claw.

—That there were, in fact, thousands of Christians in Central America, among whom must be counted those present, who had come on other ways than violence. Who were thus offering an enormous relief, both personal and political, from the "violenticizing" of life. Who, refusing to be drawn into the vortex, were creating day after day a definition of the human that surpassed the all-encompassing definitions being offered by politics and the military, definitions that, no matter how urgently pressed in the present crisis, still must be regarded as morally questionable.

—That our Christian understanding of the human must, in

such circumstances, be all the more clearly vindicated; not necessarily in words, still less in exhortation, but most of all by body language, service of others, fidelity to our symbols, discipline, and prayer. By simply staying put, despite all threats and dangers, because we believe in what we do.

—That in opposition to the omniviolence of modern war, whether a purported just war or not, something could be done. (A simple statement, but one that needed renewal day by day, in heart and hands.) What that something might be, was for those to judge who were gifted with a nuanced and long-term understanding of the situation. (In the present instance, given the presence and work of nurses, sisters, and priests, a great deal more than "something" was already being done, as could be seen.)

—That we had learned something at home, the hard way, from years of trial and error. Had learned it, moreover, at a time when the weight of a maniacal culture was laid on us to persuade us precisely that nothing could be done. When, moreover, the law intervened to warn: nothing had better be done! When prison sentences came down hard, including a three-to-ten-year sentence on the speaker; this in consequence of saying, publicly, something could be done. And of doing it. (The consequence, really, of the truth taught in liberation theology: the de facto unity of orthodoxy and orthopraxis.)

—That the discovery of tactics in a given situation was inevitably chancy. That tactics were, in any case, a secondary matter. The first being the spiritual understanding and discipline of nonviolence.

—That instant solutions, airlifted in by strangers, were roughly as palatable or nourishing as instant food mixes. Both led to a groaning in the guts. So let us eschew them.

—The point being not one of seeking solutions or brainstorming about tactics, but asking the right questions.

—Not, at the same time, making a kind of petulant vocation out of moral complexity, the code language being words like "ambiguity," "problematic," and their various etceteras. That it was the conviction (albeit an unwilling one, and often resisted within) of the speaker that complexity was not to be reveled in, but suffered on the way to moral clarity.

And so to bed, in view of a vigorous morrow.

•

Dawn brought a great rattling exodus of soldiery; it seemed in my semistupor that they were thumping in hobnails across the tile floor of my room.

Almost but not quite. My room gave on the street; so across the way, did the caserne, disquieting propinquity.

I learned that the local contingent of some two thousand soldiers was to be greatly augmented, a new camp being even then under construction just to the west of the mission. A Colonel Cruz of sanguinary repute had until recently been in charge of things military in the town. A priest filled us in: "He was one of three or four of the most cruel and wanton; given the reputation of the military, quite a distinction! He started off here at a time when the military was by no means as prominent as now. He was trying hard to integrate everyone in town into his plan. We were included; there were courteous phone calls, invitations to his 'community meetings.' He was making a great outreach, determined to normalize things as he went along, ensuring that the military took over. Very early on, we decided we had to make it clear to him that we were not included, whatever his fantasies about us, himself or the town's future. Thereupon the courtesies stopped dead; since then, it's been a standoff of sorts. But he wreaked havoc here, so many died unexplainably, there was such a level of terror, it was too much even for Duarte and the Americans. So Cruz was hustled off the scene, part of the new window dressing being that the really murderous officers would be shipped out of the country. Cruz, along with the others, ends up in clover; he's now on scholarship at the War College in Washington.

"I remember when the guerillas did a very daring, well-planned attack on his troops; a number were killed and a lot of costly sabotage done. Cruz called me in. I went along, mostly to see what the great leader looked like after such a blow. He was slumped in his chair; dispirited, he had a tape recording on, motioned me to a seat, without interrupting the tape. Do you know what he was listening to? Weird. It was a message from the guerillas, announcing the attack, the casualties and destruction, the whole bit. And Cruz was sitting there, reliving it all. Do you believe it? And for some crazy reason, he wanted me along to hear it too."

•

Had I known what the day would bring, the cost to my dorsal fin and assorted creaking bones, I surely would have reneged. However. Homerically speaking, the gods were opaque; Gene and I mounted our trusty Land Rover along with Ed the Franciscan, and off we went. To Nueva Piaqua, a mountain village further into the Land of Contention.

Mock heroic is the only appropriate style, I groaned to myself. Such a land, bristling with hostility toward the human frame, so demonic a concatenation of boulders, barely fordable gnashing streams, mud to the shin bone. Something that could be termed a road, only by the most violent and Procrustean violation of plain meaning! We held on for very life, the Rover, fitful gritty dog that it was, clenched its gears like two jaws, barked and bellowed—and made it! Whether it all but upended or turned aquatic and drank the deep, or as though on the spoor of mystery nosed on and on into the brush—through it all, we urged our steed onward with heroic groans and incantations. And finally, after two hours of more of this purgating progress (I holding for dear life on a salvific sidebar, Gene all but homogenized into prime matter in the rear seat, Ed gripping like a vise the reins of this mettlesome steed)—we made it! Like a mystical galleon of old, symbol of the questing soul, come into port out of the arm of the sea—we turned our last mountain aside. Then, with a hectic snort of an apocalyptic horse—there we were!

It was not apparent that our arrival was the Event of the Month. No flags were out; the tympana were silent. We parked beside the church; three glum villagers, including a child, were there, sitting along a wall. But the village was so silent! Almost a predawn quiet—in blazing high noon. Ed's face fell; he inquired of the sparse welcomers what might be wrong, why was no one appearing for Mass, and this the feast day of the patron saint?

Things were explained in the halting tongue of the villagers. Neuva Piaqua had changed hands again. The padre had only to look about him; since his last visit (the slogans on the walls told it), the guerrilla forces had come in and routed the army, correcting, meantime, the official scripture of town cosmology; it now read, scrawled large on walls and doors: "The militia fights for a new social and economic order!" "NO to the electoral farce; YES to the popular struggle!" "To vote is to support the intervention of the gringos!"

We had entered the village on, so to speak, a first week of creation—everything made new, chaos and its gods turned back. But as is invariably and sorrowfully true, when a new pantheon claims the earth, the votaries of the older gods suffer for it; a purge of the heterodox is inevitable. So a roundup of recalcitrants had occurred; terror charged the atmosphere. For such excellent reasons, house shutters were locked tight; up and down the blind street, the silence would twice deafen the dead.

Need it be added we were undaunted? Dangers by land, dangers by water; we were a very Pauline trio of ills and daunts overcome. Ed, still at the wheel of destiny, ordered the bells rung on the instant, the Mass prepared for. Then he entered the church, available, if by chance, a few parishioners drifted in, for preliminary shrivings.

Gene and I, meantime, moseyed about the town; no great distance to cover, since only a single road stretched ahead, cobbled, immemorial. And slogans all about; the very walls seemed to cry out a hermeneutic of purported salvation. Back and forth, as in some mad saga, the slogans erased, contradicted, corrected; the fortunes of the gods, a bloody tide bearing along, willy-nilly, the hapless mortals, resisting or adjusting, suffering the uncertain whims of the implacable and powerful; Mars, Athena, Zeus, his throne shaken; the Eumenides, the restorers of the unbalanced scales of justice.

People began to appear, against all expectation. You could see it in the faces: the church was in many senses, literal and figurative, a sanctuary. A lifting of the cloud; they unpacked their terror at the church door.

And the children, prattling, drifting about unrestrained; if they could be safe within these walls, then surely. . . . More than a hundred were present as the Mass started.

The church, a spotty, grey, unwashed barracks. Statues clothed in bizarre finery, a fixated stare behind glass, deterrent dolls of heaven. Altar accoutrements tacky as a bazaar. And then from the pews, a whine of petitionary song. Lord have mercy . . . Lord hear our prayer. . . .

And I, banishing anything of disdain or of what in another place might go by the name of outraged esthetic. Silenced under the burden of these lives, the burden of their God, whose cross, anew and anew fabricated, is laid on frail shoulders, as the innocent and ignorant are whipped along toward Golgotha.

Soldiers, the historical constant; and torture and kidnapping and justice outraged. These are the realities that like detailed peasant art (nails, thorns, ladder, sponge, rooster, Veronica's veil, superscription, skull, lance, dice, serpent) are never laid aside, not once in my lifetime declared null. . . . The Passion was the bloody central cliché of history; if I were not purblind, it was being enacted, in its malevolence, its crashing bathos, its mystery and depth, before my eyes.

How arrange one's thoughts at the spectacle unfolding here, the aura of suffering and nobility surrounding the village women, the absent men (absent being a meek word for the disappeared; it was as though their bloody outline lay on the flagstones, the third fall of Christ).

I could at least be silent and possess my soul. . . .

The village subsists through production of pottery. Toward the rear of the church, a painting by a local artist depicted a scene from Jeremiah. The text read, "As earth in the hands of the potter, so you are in My hands."

•

And so returned to Gotera, one episode inviting attention. Our driver announced we were to stop en route at the house of an old woman, and convey her to town and doctor. It transpired that in her remote dwelling, all unprotected, one night she had been beaten viciously by a deranged neighbor. So we traversed once more that broken excuse of a road and stopped at a wayside hut. She came out, bent and feeble, stick in hand, anybody's wrinkled grandmother, a kerchief framing her bruised face.

She was alert and affectionate and toothless. Introduced, she laid a hand on my arm and exclaimed delightedly: "All these priests! Now if I die on the way, what a blessing I'll have!"

She climbed aboard, we rocked along, she holding on as best she might, almost fainting with fever and weakness, Ed meantime watching her with solicitude, murmuring from time to time, "Only a little further, grandma. . . ." We arrived, the women put her to bed in the parish compound; report had it she went to sleep like a child.

I think of her, that terrible road, the sorrowful terrorized village. The plague of war, the lies and slogans, painted, painted over; corrections, denial, outrage, folly. Vote, don't vote; the gringos are liars, the National Guard deceives; believe us, don't believe them. . . . The army taking prisoners, the guerrillas taking hostages. The colonel at Mass on Sunday, all virtue and spit and polish; the colonel in a slump, totting up his losses on Monday. And the killing that never ends, the killing by either side, killing ferocious or regretted, indiscriminate or nicely calculated. And the dead; grateful in the estimate of the living, or ungrateful; having perished in good hands or bad. . . .

And then, a footnote, an aside: the act of mercy that redeems. A back road, a shack, "a life of dubious value"; the old woman. She is of little account in war, of little value in the peace that is another form of war. She neither spins nor reaps nor consumes nor shows discernible interest in any or all the foregoing. Wonderfully ignorant she is of armies and slogans (which she cannot read in any case). She has never voted (that fraudulent license, the next round of killing and plunder). She has in sum nothing to offer "the cause," having lost all to this army or that, this gun, that machete. She has lost nearly everything, as this world would account resources, valuables, possessions. But what has she kept? That was the question that intrigued and silenced us. It was her faith in us (and ours, God knew, in her)—kept indeed, in the nobility of her ignored life.

So we arrived back where we started, some eight hours later, to hear at table the sagas of our valiant compañeros. . . . And in due course, after warm farewells, to take our leave.

•

I summon up, with what a sense of poignant gratitude, the faces around that table. These occur to me: ardor, urbanity, charm, sanity, goodness, irony, patience, hospitality, good deeds indifferent to public note, modesty of demeanor, face to face courage. Come hell or blown up bridges. Indeed, to tempt a fact into metaphor, these sisters and priests long before burned their secure bridges behind.

And so to the airport, our driver Ed warning us mildly that he drove more concentratedly if not obliged to converse. I properly grew silent. Then a few kilometers on, with precision, almost with forethought, he struck in its gaunt rear flank a vagrant calf, sent it bawling beefily after its cow. Whereupon, concluding evidently that such a cure was worse than the ill, we undertook normal converse once more.

•

Back in San Salvador, and a meeting with the vicar of the diocese, a kind of assistant to the archbishop. He could have been appointed successor to Romero, we were informed, but declined; knowing beyond doubt that he would shortly thereafter appear on some death list. We could see why; a figure in black, dark eyes gleaming with intelligence, the unrehearsed language of one who speaks his mind.

He had just returned from the Honduran camps, visiting the thousands of displaced, saying Mass for them. He spoke sorrowfully of the Honduran plans to move the exiles some six hundred kilometers inland; in order, he concluded, to clear the frontier across which El Salvador could be invaded.

He spoke of Romero, under whom he had served. Said: simply, he was a saint, rather old-fashioned in his piety, but intelligent, a great student, an inveterate reader of theology. His homilies so electrified the country, national affairs halted when he spoke from the altar. "You know, in Salvador, everyone, even the very poor, have radios. . . . Moreover, his was the only news available to us, and he gave it fearlessly every week. Everything was strictly censored, there was no one else with the resources or the courage to speak out about what was happening. Then after Mass, he would walk in procession to the rear of the cathedral, and answer questions from the media. You see how all these activities made him a marked man.

"A very simple piety, but unmistakable. One time I remember, we had a meeting with the cardinal and a member of the junta. Toward the end of the meeting Romero left the room suddenly. I went looking for him after a few minutes, as the guests were about to depart. I found him in the chapel; he had felt the discussion was at such an impasse there was nothing else to do but pray. . . .

"When we went to his little house to collect things after his death, I found in the little table by his bed a discipline and chain, the instruments of penance you Jesuits had taught him." (This with a smile)

•

> The god of money forces us
> to turn our backs
> on the God of Christianity.
> Because people want a god
> who turns his back on them,
> instead of the true God—
> therefore many criticize the church.
> They kill every movement
> that tries to destroy false idols
> and give us the true God.
>
> Oscar Romero

•

None of us were willing to leave Salvador without improvising a Romero pilgrimage. So, by way of a start, we trekked to the cathedral.

Unfinished, austere, it might have been beautiful, but for the memories; color it black, color it red: black for mourning, red for murder. One enters, one grows lightheaded; a building that draws to itself such catastrophe; a cave of contrary murderous winds. At right angles across the square juts the bombastic colonial front of the Presidential Palace; from its roof had erupted the shots that provoked deadly panic at Romero's funeral.

The interior of the cathedral: all good intentions, tacky outcome. As thought the architects, every skill at command, were dismissed, replaced by hacks with contrary orders. As though the replacements were known as the Cosmeticians of Saint Sulpice. . . .

Romero had, in fact, issued the command that halted the construction. He announced summarily that the building would be finished only when every citizen of Salvador was decently housed. Thus did faith come down hard, as Kierkegaard declared it must, on esthetics.

We entered throught the transept door. The cramped odoriferous street; then as though entering Aladdin's cave after despoilment. I breathed deep, startled, even stupefied; the shock of airy space, pure depth and height. So un-Spanish, so unpresidential, so uncolonialized.

In a tiny country, hardly larger than one of our counties at home, where, moreover, neither Indian nor Spanish art had made any great impact, where it is difficult today to come on artifacts of character—someone had indeed achieved a breakthrough. It lives in the noble lines and splendid proportions; it lives alone.

Since the bare shell was deemed unfit for worship, it was fitted out somehow, a piece here, an afterthought there, slapped together. A plywood reredos insults the altar; above, a globe and a Christ contend. Haste and no waste. In the transept, we came on Romero's tomb.

Alive or dead, here was the clue to any understanding of Salvador. Alive, dead, there played about his form the twin lightnings of holiness and social turmoil. They lit up the era; he was the wick of the flame. He fed the flame and it destroyed him. And that, from the point of view of conventional tyranny, was the end of it. The insult was heard around the world; the slamming shut of a dossier.

But tyranny, that blind blunderer, was seldom in such gross error. Some other sound was shortly heard worldwide, a shudder, both of mourning and outrage. The dossier would not remain closed. It opened partially, irreversibly, as though by a law of its own. It whispered like a ghost volume; something ominous, of crime and consequence; an unexampled sign of the persistence of memory, soul, sanctity. Like the moon tipping the tides, the presence and palpable influence of spirit.

I wanted to pray at his tomb, a simple matter. As I would want to pray at the tomb of Martin King, or Dorothy Day; the former because he, like the archbishop, survived for awhile to do extraordinary work in a witless and bizarre world. And Dorothy, because she, like the archbishop, knew that injustice and violence are wreaked first of all on the poor of the world—whose plight, contrary to common belief, is no creation of God, but of our "rotten filthy system," as she put things so pithily.

I wanted to pray for friends at home, possessed as I am of a nearly childish confidence in the saints—a confidence born perhaps of near despair that we mortals, unaided, will never undo the bloody mess of the world.

We knelt there like Chaucer's motley pilgrims, at our Canterbury shrine, this uninviting impregnable tomb, imbedded like a time capsule in our mad century. It was festooned with messages, banners, all manner of plaques and grisly cutouts of limbs restored. It was like skywriting on the air, like tattooing on the body of creation. Even in death, he gave voice to the voiceless. Their cry: all honor to the fallen one, veneration to Romero, the loser in the great chancy lottery of tyranny!

The cathedral is, as Joan Didion wrote, the clearest political statement in Salvador. This being admitted, how is one to characterize the tomb? Pope John Paul, no mean political figure, was by all accounts unimpressed by Romero. On the occasion of the papal visit to Salvador, he visited the tomb only privately and in passing. The practice of *Romanità,* one concludes, does not require such personages as Romero. In life they were better played down; and in death, their vindication by way of sainthood will be long in coming. But such reflections are perhaps beside the point; which is, after all, the perduring phenomenon; Romero and his people, in life and death. It would be redundant, even idle, to report that for millions of citizens, he is already a saint. The news is out. He is revered as such, invoked as such; a living presence, requiring no foreign intervention or encouragement, even of the highest.

•

Dennis was insistent; we must also visit the chapel where Romero was shot. So we sought out the Hospital for the Incurables.

Through the gates, up a hill verdant with spring foliage, to an altogether neat and attractive place.

The chapel was undistinguished, conventional modern; that is to say, it strained after a style, and achieved only a monumental accumulation of brass, marble, and paint. Angles were sharp, paint vigorously applied in unlikely combinations. An unlikely scene altogether, for an event that shook the world.

The message of the killers was conveyed with the cleanness and finality of a bullet; if the bishop could be murdered at the Mass, what scene indeed could be named a sanctuary, who was safe, and where? A universal message indeed, in mockery of the universal church: Beware, in modern war everyone, regardless of station, age, merit, is fair meat.

The truth surrounding Romero's death is badly served, I believe, by recourse to theories of conspiracy or extra-governmental anarchy. The truth lies nearer home, anyone's home; a home truth so to speak. Which is to say, the warmaking state (a term which reality today renders redundant) *is* the conspiracy, such authority is by nature anarchic. Such authority as then held Salvador in its grip (and still does) could not for long survive if Romero did. It was as simple and brutal as that. . . .

The Mass of the archbishop was underway, the chapel door lay open in the clement weather. The sharpshooter, a black clad hellion out of Cocteau's inferno, zoomed in. Romero stood at the altar, facing his sparse congregation of nuns and layfolk. One shot sufficed; he fell in his bloodied vestments, dead on the instant. The gunman revved up, disappeared. It is stale news that several years later he has never been apprehended; nor is there evidence that he was ever seriously sought; nor, indeed, is it likely that if apprehended he would make clear whether the inspiration for the deed, or its motive, initiated in him.

The reasons for all this need not detain us. The murder of the archbishop, like any flagrant crime, does not occur at the whim, or at the serious initiation, of this or that gunman. Powers other than the murderer decreed the crime; decreed as its necessary adjunct that its trail be allowed to cool, until it is all but obliterated. (And as to promises, currently made, that the case is to be opened once more—we shall see.)

We stood silent at the chapel entrance; a nun approached us.

Would we wish to visit the house of Romero? Gene was delighted; this was a rare privilege, the house being in custody of the sisters, and seldom opened to outsiders for any reason. . . .

I sensed his excitement, I could in no way partake of it, being less than enamored with visits to the dwellings of the formerly living. The reluctance is no doubt instinctive, beyond reasonableness; some obscure feeling that I do not belong in the precincts; almost an awe in the presence of a very absence.

When a death has brought great personal loss, my reluctance becomes almost insuperable. And at that moment, the death of Romero, the brute incalculable fact, obliterated all lingering curiosity—to encounter his ghost, or even his ghostly walls and garden. I hastened my steps through the rooms, and exited again, as quickly as decently possible. . . .

A tidal wave of memory, as I stood there amid the hospital traffic. I was back at Merton's monastery, some eight years after his death. The monks had invited a group of friends, scholars, poets to pass a day there, in course of workshops and discussions on Merton's life and writings. It was the first time I could trust myself to return.

One feature of the visit was a walk through the Kentucky woods, to Merton's hermitage; there we were invited to tour and tarry, to read the poetry of the renowned hermit. Or otherwise, as we might choose, to pass the autumn afternoon, bathed in haze and monastic quiet.

I chose the otherwise. Atavistic beyond doubt. But I could not bear to linger in those rooms, where friendship had flowered, spontaneous and hilarious at once; where an unbreakable thread was spun, a lifeline I still held in hand. Those unlikely monastic hours could not, for all of longing, be summoned back, could scarcely even be spoken of.

I wandered alone in the woods, ablaze with gold. In the cottage, Bob Lax, Merton's hermit friend returned from Greece for the occasion, read in his understated monotone selections from Merton's late poems. It was the plangent voice of autumn, hovering over the hazy fields of goldenrod, ragweed, honeysuckle. And the reality lay heavy on me; Merton was gone, and why should I trick and mistreat my soul, like a halloween ghost; as though, at times, in certain moods (the summer, dying like a splendid phoenix), as though death and loss do not presume and preempt nearly all of life? Marveling, the guests moved through the cottage. Nothing was disturbed: fireplace, ikons, the desk and its books. And in the inner room, the narrow cot and its woven coverlet. . . .

And in Romero's house, two or three small rooms, a celibate neatness and order. A few changes were obvious; his portrait hung in the entrance; most of his books were removed by his family. And on the cot lay an inert, moving symbol, the wooden crozier of the fallen shepherd.

•

Dennis was a great one for reminding us of unfinished business. We had not yet stopped at the Jesuit high school, though we had spent much time with the university community. Might not this be taken as a neglect of one, in favor of the more prestigious other? We hastened to repair matters.

And altogether to our advantage. We were greeted warmly; a priest immediately offered himself as guide. We walked toward an impressive, even splendid building, set in a vast courtyard. A thousand students, we were informed, were enrolled: "Not many of the rich, you understand; we are out of favor since certain events were precipitated here."

Understatement again, the protective coloration of survivors. Our tour was conducted in the same spirit, a dignified impersonality, as though we were being enlightened as to events long past, or third-person occurrences. Thus: "It was from this room [he opened a door giving on the court] from here the Guardia Civil seized the young leaders of the political opposition. Their bodies were found later that night; they had been tortured and executed."

And were you present on that day?

"Yes. In there [a gesture toward the lobby] they ordered us to stretch out on our faces. One of them stood guard over us with a machine gun, the others rounded up the youths."

And what happened to the Jesuit community afterward?

"We realized that in light of everything we could expect the worst. After all, we had offered these young men a place to meet. The police knew this; a matter to them of plain sedition. So we decided within hours to leave the house, fade into a barrio for some months. Meantime, many students washed their hands of us; not only had matters hottened up, but our choices, which I prefer to call ethical, but were commonly stigmatized as political, were now evident to all. After five days, the house we had vacated was seized by the police. We lived with the terror for a long time, in dispersion. But now [with a dismissing shrug] things are fairly normal for this country."

•

There was yet another piece of unfinished business, hardly in our control. It came by way of a phone message; a decision had been reached at last in the Griffiss Plowshares case. A split decision as to alleged crimes: not guilty of sabotage, not guilty of conspiring to sabotage; guilty of destruction of government property, guilty of conspiring to destroy government property.

•

> Our action, trial, jail even, are not cures;
> they are attempts to free ourselves
> from the civility that kills.
> This trial was another example of
> good manners
> good missiles
> good night.
>
> Karl Smith,
> Griffiss Plowshares

•

A mixed verdict, received with mixed emotion. As always, a sense of relief; things could have been worse. . . . An implied definition of our world?

I thought wryly, a definition indeed; one that ought to be included in a post-Vatican post-Hiroshima catechism; sic.

Q: Why, dear children, did God make the world the way it is?

A: Dear adult, God did not make the world the way it is. We made the world the way it is; which is to say, and not to put too fine a point on things—you did.

(The tone of the next question becomes somewhat nettled.)

Q: Then what part does God play in the world?

A: Dear adult, but for the patience of God, our world would be in a far worse state than it presently endures. Thus God's part, given us, is largely one of mitigation and patience. And can only be termed major.

Salvadoran woman (San José Guayabal, El Salvador)

Refugee camp at Santa Tecla (El Salvador)

List of martyrs in the
Church of San Francisco
(Mejicanos, El Salvador)

Billboard from taxi
(San Salvador, El Salvador)

The bridge at San Miguel (Morazán Province, El Salvador)

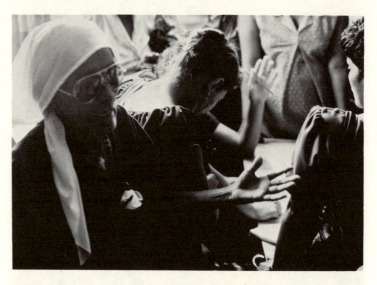

The Committee of Mothers and Families of Political Prisoners, Disappeared, and Assassinated of El Salvador (San Salvador, El Salvador)

Destroyed power station
(Ocotal, Nicaragua)

Campesino
(Santa Maria, Nicaragua)

3
Hymn to the New Humanity

(Nicaragua, El Salvador, and the U.S. June, 1984)

The guns are common as stacked firewood, and as cheap.
They are common as walking sticks carried by the aged and infirm.
There is a gun for every contra who carries a gun.
There are toy guns for infants and flowery guns for little girls.
To the delight of children, there are clown guns that go !popopop!—and wouldn't harm an insect.
There are chocolate guns for Easter; guns that spout water and guns that sprout a parasol for rainy days.
The guns of course have eyes. The guns of the Guardia Civil have ears. And there are merchant guns that smell a dollar, like a miser's nose in a sirocco of money.
And statesmen's guns, equipped with silencers, sheathed like their owners in raw silk, a spiffy outfit.

There is a rare gun, a gun of dark rumor. The ultimate gun, the gun named god. Like god, it has never been seen; in virtue of the invisibility, it must be believed in.
Somewhere, no one knows where, whether on land or sea or in the air, this gun is sequestered, stroked, nourished by the hands of servitors.
Like the queen bee of hell, it waxes in the dark; fed on morsels of children, boiled eyes and pickled ears. It is indifferently a carnivore, a florivore, a faunivore.

This is a metaphysical gun. It renders all other guns, together with their makers and users, redundant.
It is aimed at the heart of history, the secret wellsprings of life.

Innocent as the three famous monkeys, guns see no evil, speak no evil.
Guns believe in guns, guns hope in guns, guns adore guns. In the new dispensation, these are honored as theological virtues.
There are loving marital guns. They vow fidelity, each to the other, at the altar of revolution. Thereupon they are blessed by clerical guns in white surplices.
Also guns are laid on the table at Mass, next to the bread and wine; then they are said to be consecrated guns.
There are guns held by sheep and guns held by goats. To the former Christ says: Come ye blessed. To the others: Depart from me. Or so it is said.
In El Salvador, the guardia peer out from behind the smoked windows of vans, like Mississippi sheriffs behind their shades; the look of a leveled gun.
In Nicaragua, the guns have learned to smile; like cornucopias of metal, they whisper promises: Dear children, trust us; from our barrels pour the *ABC's,* medicines, a blessed life. Trust us, stroke us, vote for us. In our dark void is concealed all your future.

It has proved embarrassing on occasion that the Christian documents are recusant on this matter of guns. Exegetes, artists, poets, intellectuals have been moved in consequence, to create as it were, a contrary hypothesis. The empty-handed Christ, they declare, "would have," "must have," "might have" carried a gun. Or at the least, he favored their legitimate use; just guns for just causes.
In the older iconography, the hands of Christ are by no means empty. They bear the bounteous fruit of a storied imagination: shepherd's staff, teacher's scroll, a lamb or two, wheat, chalice. Now these

sublime and simple things are lifted from his hands. Even that bloody heart, livid as a skinned plum, to which his index pointed as a very *sigillum* of love— it is torn from his side.

We have in fact imagined a better way of imagining him than he was capable of.

What has occurred is roughly this. There came a time when it was no longer possible to venerate the older symbols of the holy and human. Our species evolved, in accord with exigencies of time and place.

A new human emerged from the tired womb of tradition; a tradition which here and there, through service of lip and heart, had preached a cult of—gunlessness.

A gauche ideology indeed! On its behalf, believers failed to coin a usable term. Nonviolence? It was a clumsy transliteration. They were gunless, that is all.

Our own times signaled a breakthrough. Guns were no longer mere instruments of bleak choice. They were now simply a matter of wholeness, morphology. To this point, to be born gunless corresponded, in the ethical sphere, to a mishap in nature; an armless or legless or sightless being; one lacking in a substantial component of the human.

Thus, to bring a long matter around, a fresh light is cast on a very old subject.

Meantime, it must be admitted that a few recalcitrant priests and their sequences spurned the light. In public places they intemperately cried out the old credo to their gunless god. They were dealt with, summarily.

Our genetic leap postulated a new ikon. The older images had died with their god. They were best buried, once for all.

In this matter we were relentless: new humans, a new god.

Our theology produced a generation, not of iconoclasts, but of inspired entrepreneurs. We now possess, in plazas and shadowy corners, in discourse and dance, the Christ we have come so richly to deserve.

4
Nicaragua

And so by air, the following morning, into Nicaragua. A matter, so sudden as to be explosive, of night into day. The contrast could not be missed, on the instant, as we came in. Soldiers all about the airport, as expected. Still, there are soldiers and soldiers: soldiers of night and of day. And these had a daylight look, indeed a very noonday look. As though, according to the biblical text, their works could endure the scrutiny of day; or of conscience, or the law. They stood about the airport in purposeful ease; as though they belonged where they stood, normal, part of the nature of things.

They were armed of course (the "of course" being added unhappily, a concession to the lapsed nature of things), but the arms were borne as though they were stage property, by no means for use, except in dire crisis. Certainly not for the use they were put to, day after day, in Salvador, the indiscriminate bloody whim. In the military, a different mien and bearing. No menace, no necessity of taking the long way round. We were to see it again and again, soldiers and police at ease with the people.

"And why not?" we were questioned in turn when we chanced to remark on this. "They are after all our soldiers; they are pledged to defend us; they come from our families. How could they act as our enemies? . . . "

Peggy Sherer of the New York Catholic Worker movement was on the spot to welcome us. And what a good beginning it was! We knew of her through the New York network. How she had joined the Witness for Peace early on, and had become one of the coordinators of that effort, helping orientate new groups of North Americans as they arrived, standing with them in the endangered northern towns of Nicaragua, where the menace of the contras was greatest.

She had news for us. An interracial group of North Americans had arrived in Managua that day. The junta, in a special gesture of welcome, was even then meeting with the group in a seminary nearby. Would we like to attend?

Fed up as we were with political medicine men and their hype, unaccustomed to candor in high places, we agreed, sensing this might be an occasion to see a new politics in action.

And were, to a point, not disappointed. Under the lights and the grinding cameras sat the government, junta and cabinet.

We were witnessing a weekly event, in the course of which the junta appeared in one or another barrio, to face the people. In principle, the exchange was wide open, any and all questions addressed.

The security, considering the situation nationally, the contra and CIA attacks, the very real possibility of assassination—it could only be termed ludicrous. We arrived in the area, were questioned once as to our business, and were waved forward. That was all. That evening, it was not campesinos or workers or students who were invited to question the government, but the newly arrived delegation. Considering everything—the international press and TV, the presence of some two hundred attentive citizens—I judged that the obstacles against candor were formidable.

As for the northerners, with exceptions, they acquitted themselves creditably. Their situation, too, could hardly be termed an easy one. They were guests, newly arrived; their host country was menaced, invaded, sabotaged by the U.S. government. They might have settled in consequence for a policy of praise and stroking. A few of them did. But for the most part, their questioning was straightforward, even blunt. (My sympathy for the visitors was instinctive. Arriving as I had in Hanoi in 1968, with North Vietnam under merciless assault, I faced a like dilemma: Was I entitled to question closely or criticize the conduct of a government waging a war of bare survival against the juggernaut? The dilemma was to haunt me, and others, for years.)

Question (the questioner a young black): "I introduce myself as a teacher from Boston. I was also a conscientious objector during the Vietnam War. I understand that presently there is a law of universal military service in Nicaragua. I should like to know whether the law offers provision for objectors of conscience. . . . "

The fire was hot, the fat was in it.

In sum (and after lengthy analysis of the differences between military service on behalf of the U.S. in Vietnam and serving in defense of Nicaragua), the conclusion was austere, to say the least: There was, indeed there could be, no provision for those who, for whatever reason, would not bear arms for the country. Indeed, the response hinted strongly, of late, large numbers presenting themselves demanding this special treatment; both their numbers and the tardiness of their appeal gave cause for healthy skepticism. . . .

I received the news with a sinking spirit. Provision for conscience, even in desperate circumstances—what else summed up the implicit claim of the revolution, which defined itself, in fact, as a revolution of conscience? And more, had verified the claim in ways that won the admiration of so many, in ways that brought hope to us also—that even in North America, something new could be born, in the image of Nicaragua.*

Question (a native North American): "We have read and heard a great deal about the situation of the Miskito Indians of the Atlantic coast. Their treatment is, I believe, the only aspect of the revolution which has earned the critical scrutiny of Amnesty International. We hear of preventive detention, uprooting from the land, mistreatment in jail of a number of leaders. You are undoubtedly aware of the historical crimes committed against my people by the U.S. government. There is, in consequence, intense interest with regard to the native peoples in your country. . . . "

The answer, alas, fell far short of satisfaction. Nor indeed did it, in my opinion, exhibit a sense of responsibility.

---

*I am happy to be able to modify the above, in light of information received from a friend. According to Gustavo Parrajon, head of CEPAD (an organization of the forty or more Protestant churches in Nicaragua), an arrangement has been reached with the government, with regard to objectors of conscience. On application, a youth who is a church member may, with the supporting testimony of his pastor, be granted the status of conscientious objector. The government, according to Parrajon, is reluctant to recognize that option formally in the law, for several reasons, including its effect on the military and on those whose relatives have been killed. Also to be considered is the political issue—exacerbated by the bishops of Nicaragua—of military service.

If I single out this query, which Ernesto Cardenal rose to deal with, it was not only because he temporized, or undertook a lengthy laudatory paean, the accomplishments of "us" in regard to "them" (from the start, his language made one wince). But more. His words seemed to me a betrayal of his cause. His cause, which was, in principle, our own. For if the Nicaraguan Revolution was to offer hope, either to its own people or to the world at large, it seemed to me that the offering must include a special sensitivity toward the truth.

It was a question indeed that could not be confined to Nicaragua; it reverberated throughout the world, first, second, third: Could there be a government that did not lie or equivocate or conceal its intentions—intentions that were of life and death import to the governed?

Everyone present, I judge, was conscious of the obstacles facing a government under siege. Everyone, beginning with the junta, also knew that the revolutionary government had made serious mistakes. It was common knowledge; it was inevitable; it was human nature. What new government (let alone old government) did not make mistakes, some of them due to the incompetence and clumsiness of those newly empowered, others being grievous, malicious, deliberate matters of policy?

The duty, indeed the hope, was truthfulness. Cardenal's language was particularly offensive in this regard. He admitted no mistakes; the question of reparation or correction was therefore rendered null. Yet we knew, I venture everyone in the room knew, something of the "mistakes" for which the government was responsible—a charitable word indeed, to convey the reality of the Indians' grievances. Witnesses had written and spoken of such matters, in the U.S. and elsewhere; such matters could be separated out from propaganda, on whatever side.

I sensed a strange *déjà écouté*. I was hearing a language, a style, all too familiar. I will risk being odious in saying so. "We" and "they" were keystones of the vocabulary of federal racism in the U.S. Such language was in use almost invariably, and at least by implication, when Reagan ventured to speak of the poor or of blacks. "We" and "they" were all but members of separate species, dwelling in separate worlds, we donors and benefactors, they the lowly beneficiaries. Thus class divisions harden into political attitudes and methods, whether in the U.S. or Nicaragua.

My language here is admittedly severe. I can only plead that it stems from disappointed hope. It is one tactic, and a debatable one, to have recourse to special pleading, to sidestep a serious question, for whatever reason—because the media are in attendance, voracious and vigilant at once, or because one is a member of government, and there is an official line to be hewn to. . . . But it seems to me a far more serious matter to divide a national populace, no matter what its ethnic variety, into haves and have nots. More, to imply that a government is the executor and perpetuator of this "arrangement of nature."

Cardenal, by such language, presents himself as an implicit ideologue of the revolution. He presents the revolution as a kind of absolute platonic form, beyond question or critique. Essentially his is a romantic view, apparently untroubled by the troublesome facts of human fallibility. The view is also curiously old hat. It is as though under the mufti, beret, poncho, there beat the pulse of an unreconstructed amicus curiae.

I have tried to express elsewhere my friendship with Ernesto Cardenal, my respect for his courage, for the difficult path he walks. But it must be said that he tries friendship sorely. I write this, realizing it is possibly a good thing that friends disagree, and say so; even publicly, if that proves useful. But it is another matter, for example, to quote Merton, without evidence, as a supporter of revolutionary violence; to "quote" Gandhi (a quote Cardenal has been unable to verify) as, on occasion, supporting violence; and to stigmatize North American pacifists as "stubborn and stupid" folk who live "in another world."

•

We were received in due course by Cardenal at the Ministry of Culture. The meeting was marked, as will be noted later, by politesse and little more. Photos were taken, courtesies and small talk exchanged. For my part, sensing that our positions remained unchanged, I felt no urge to launch into an old, inevitably hot discussion. The time was not apt. Whether it would become so at a later date, neither of us so much as ventured to speculate.

I feel a great sadness when I think of Cardenal. Not so much in view of the ambiguity under which he must live in the church (who of us does not so live?). But because he is—victimized, a fixed star of revolution, so regarded and feted in Europe and North America. A symbol indeed, and, through no fault of his own, an extremely ambiguous one in the eyes of the symbol-makers—a kind of substitute for the unresolved violence of the affluent (even of affluent Christians) who love blood sports, but perhaps no sport so well as the distancing and projecting on another of the violent vision of revolution. A revolutionary fantasy, need it be added; an upheaval that will bring change in every direction— except their own.

Priest revolutionary! Two strikes in a game which allows only three, did Ernesto but know the rules. The first, called by Rome; the second by western culture—a culture that celebrates its heroes, even while it dreads and resists serious change. Indeed, that makes of heroes both surrogates and victims.

•

We were warmly received by the Jesuits, a small team of specialists dwelling in a pair of diminutive, neighboring houses, a patch of green in the midst. Peter Marchetti, a U.S. priest, heads the enterprise, if such a term is useful in describing so unassuming a man. They crowd three visitors in somehow (I in the corner of a "common room" together with a Ping-Pong table three times the size of the cot). Everyone, in one way or another, moves over to accommodate the arrivals.

Peter is in charge of land reform; he works only indirectly for the government, his chief responsibility being to the United Nations. Ferdinand Cardenal heads the literacy programs. (His achievement is nothing short of brilliant; illiteracy has all but vanished in four years, some hundred thousand young teachers volunteering for work among the campesinos. He also shortly becomes the center of a storm, invited to join the junta as minister of education. Rome objects, and strongly.)

The regimen of the house is fairly simple: early rise, departure for work, return at noon for the main meal when possible. Work again, late afternoon to late night. Once a week, liturgy on the patio at 10 P.M. And once a month, everyone repairs to the country for weekend retreat and respite.

Our arrival signaled a spontaneous welcome on the patio. Drinks were produced, discussion shortly arose as to the disposition of our days in Nicaragua. It developed that a compañero, a parish priest, had arrived from Ocotal: a Padre Antonio, tall, saturnine, thin as a pine pole, irrepressibly cheerful, trilingual (at least). His suggestion: that we accompany him on the morrow, to his home base, there to taste, in all it sulfurous reality, the war zone and the contras.

It was the evening of June 13; we turned matters about in the gentle, flower-laden air of night. Just thirteen days before, Ocotal had been savagely attacked before dawn by six hundred contras, descending like wolves on the fold from the mountains of Honduras. We would therefore be arriving in a stricken city—concerning which more later. In any case, given such an invitation, and in spite of the exhaustion that rode our bones, our wobbly land legs—who could refuse?

So we gather in the morning for departure. The event is immediately photographed, in disconcerting detail, by a wild and wooly Jesuit from Oregon, a guest in the house. He has gotten it into his head that this is an occasion of note (it is all news to us). He bounds and flits around the Land Rover, unnervingly, a house dog unleashed. He impedes, he pleads—just one more!

In due time we are underway. Antonio has us speedily out of town, launched like an arrow on the Pan American Highway. He drives and smokes and talks, a cultured Basque, a *caudillo* to the fingertips. It develops that he entered the Jesuits as a diocesan priest in Spain, and recently completed the final year of formation in Europe. A terrible year, terrible, he repeated with fervor, eyes on the road, talking through his cigarette smoke. Glad to be back in Nicaragua where he belonged, where life made some sense.

A short stop in Estelí for lunch with friends, then onward to our destination, arriving toward evening. It was a night those bound by the north can only dream of: honeyed flowers in bloom, the air suave as a velvet glove. We pull into the classic square of the old city: cathedral, governor's residence, colonial heroes brooding in the park statuary. Time, like our Land Rover, comes to an abrupt halt. We have landed, for a loony moment, in the very Empire of Nostalgia, its architecture intact, its spell unbroken.

For a moment only. I shake my head free of its intoxications, like a land creature shaking the salt of the sea. We are in a besieged city whose people, struck silent under the moon, have but recently buried their dead. The war descends; they are all but beaten under. On the face of the dead and the tormented living, the light of the moon falls like a rain of lotus petals, an enchantment, a lying comfort. Come alive, awaken!

•

Dennis is energetic and enterprising at once. No one is a stranger for long. His Spanish, though strictly improvisational, gets through. He beguiles words from anyone at hand, tries out his patois, his English, gesticulates, anything. I am dilatory, my eyes are my only curious faculty. But I comfort myself with the thought: set down what you see; others will see it too.

What I see, in the deceptive moon-charged calm of night and parting the light like a clinging curtain, is—what stands incongruously before us. A plain box of a house, the species of dwelling Jesuits slap together anywhere in the world, out of some mysterious blueprint. It is a house dictated by impatience and indifference to all comfort, a house that is hardly a house at all, more like Teresa of Avila's "uncomfortable inn, apt for a night's stay." One could hardly imagine Benedictines or Trappists dwelling in such utter, deliberate, all but contemptuous disregard for amenities. Not a square of green grass for relief; the building like a series of packing cartons set down randomly; plumbing and wiring strung through like an afterthought. As though someone had remarked idly on the absence of such; and the day following, they appeared, clumsily installed, a pipe here, a wire there; for appearance' sake rather than for comfort. The kitchen is haphazard, the cuisine unenterprising. But the welcome could only be called gargantuan; it nullified all else. A guest room, fitted for two, was available, we were informed. The third, myself, would repose in the church sacristy, some blocks distant.

So we went out into the night, the padre superior and myself, to claim my reposeful turf. He was a large wooly man with a comforting paunch; he made a gliding ecclesiastical progress through the sleepy town, raising his right hand from time to time in a restrained greeting and benediction. It was like the passing of a palanquin on wheels; and I trotted alongside like a small boy in a feast day procession.

We came into the cathedral square; at the hour nearing midnight, it was populated with sleepers. They were the campesinos of the neighboring estates, come to celebrate the Mass with their bishop on the morrow.

"They have come, many of them, a great distance, and barefoot," the padre explained in his impassive voice. "They are the *comunidades de base* of our diocese. The women and children [the padre unlocking the sacristy door] will sleep within, in the room adjoining your own."

We passed in semidarkness through a series of barracks, meeting rooms for catechism, storage spaces for musty books and images discarded. Finally to arrive at my sleeping space, a narrow, cluttered sort-of-room defined by a half partition. The only furnishing, a massive Japanese motorcycle, sundry shelves piled helter-skelter with old periodicals and miscellany; a cot, ruptured springs, a blanket and pillow; and just beyond the door, a john with discordant, unreliable plumbing.

I could hear in the night the uneasy slumber of the peasant children and their mothers. (It recalled to me the night shelter for homeless women in our neighborhood in New York—the sleepless haunted by a nightmarish tomorrow.)

On the sacristy wall, in a room giving on the street, I was to note on the morrow a poster; it pictured a couple who might qualify as the patron saint of the base communities. Husband and wife, tortured and murdered by the contras in 1983. Their son, it transpired, was mayor of Ocotal. In the recent assault the townspeople, enraged at the swath of murder, were hot after revenge. But the mayor forbade any such thing; the wounded contras, moreover, were given the same medical attention as the casualties of the city. Two new martyrs for our pondering. These, and the inevitable photos of Romero, the four nuns, Rutilio Grande, Guadalupe Carney. That rude wall! It held a weight of tragic glory . . . .

Up betimes, infantile wailing and mewing, the consumptive waterworks, the murmur of the swelling crowds outside. What a spectacle awaited the early sun! On the square were converging from adjacent streets hundreds of women, men, children, rude crosses aloft, a chant of litanies and prayers. The bishop was awaited, and a ceremony of note, the closing of the Holy Year. So joyous an occasion, it required considerable effort of mind to recall the facts of life: the city and its outlying areas so shortly before victimized by a murderous assault. Was I witnessing the speedy recovery possible to a people of faith, witnessing a rite of healing, touching with compassion wounds of grief and loss?

They sang and sang under the merciless sun; women and men in mourning, tomahawk features, endurance, survival.

And then the parting of the crowd like the parting of the sea; a few elderly, attended ladies, grand in mantillas and black, making their stately way to favored positions about the outdoor altar. They were the sparse remnant of the colonial families, dwelling grandly in walled villas adjacent to the cathedral. The bishop arrived, the ritual began. It included ceremonies special to the occasion. Three times, like a sacred truncheon, the crozier rose, struck at the portal and fell. At the third blow, as though some deity, majestic and impatient, were demanding entrance, the doors swung wide, the human tide entered like a flame into a flue. Seats had been pushed and piled in the transepts; there was standing room only.

Then singing, antiphons, litanies interminable, three hours in all. A vociferous homily, exhorting to obedience and devotion. (An exhortation that seemed, in the main, somewhat redundant. Indeed, the bishop might be led to reflect, facing as he did some two thousand exemplary and obedient souls, that he was offered that morning a corporate example of the virtues commended.)

But to the inner ear, an ear of expectation, mourning, and surmise, the silence, the omissions thundered like judgment. Every worshiper was alive and hearkening, the church was like a vortex of the Spirit. There was a homily (and yet—there was an antihomily); convictions were uttered regarding Pentecost, Spirit, church; down the aisles the doctrines marched like squads in exquisite formation. And all the while, there was omission, hiatus.

The bishop spoke at length, and fervently—about everything except life and death. It was as though, for very shame of so shameful a God, page after page of anguish and glory were torn from the Gospel.

This I am convinced must be recorded, even at risk of rhetoric.

The bishop's words hovered in the air, a mime of the event of Pentecost, a partial Pentecost at best. Not once did he touch our brows with flame, no great wind stirred the house. He was content to refer, at one point, to something so harmless and heartless as "peace in our time." That was all.

And all the while, in the eyes of worshipers, in their serious stolidity, in the grip of their hands on crosses and devotional beads, there lay the evidence of fresh grief, the loss of loved ones, the destruction of crops and livelihood.

Is it possible that the bishop knew all this, and chose not to respond? It is possible. It is also possible that a visiting pope could hear (as he had in Managua in 1983) the cries of mothers of the newly dead—and not respond. Indeed, this has assumed the blind force of a truism: in our world all things, even the most terrible, are possible. . . .

The service neared its end. The bishop called the roll of the base communities. The people raised a sea of hands; the leaders raised the crosses. In turn, room somehow made for them, each group walked toward the altar to receive a blessing, then turned and marched out, to the applause of the congregation.

We stood outside once more; the noon was perfect as a suspended jewel.

Sandino's silhouette for background; and peering about like a ship's figurehead, the ugly, bullish statue of a monsignor, its plaque commemorating "forty years of service to our people, service material and spiritual, demanding this honor. . . . "

It had been a remarkably free and uninhibited gathering of what is referred to, here and abroad, as "the persecuted church of Nicaragua." (We learned a few days later that Edward Kennedy had launched a philippic against the Sandinistas—the U.S. reaction to the Nicaraguan bishops' urging a "dialogue with all parties. . . .")

•

In Ocotal, two hundred members of the citizens' militia keep the night watch against the contras. The city is crucial to the enemy strategy, which failed in 1982 to take Jalapa, to the north, and establish a contra government there. (This purposed government, hypothetical and shadowy at once, was to be accorded immediate recognition by the U.S., a previously established and premature recognition, as things turned out.) A Jesuit conveyed us by jeep to the edge of town. We came out of the night into a large open-sided shed, lit by a single miserable bulb; the place had the look of an abandoned classroom in the tropics. (I thought of Hanoi in 1968, of Beirut in 1975, of Belfast in 1981. Self-defense, a last ditch morality of violence.)

The militia were exhausted and unwashed. They had kept more than two weeks of night vigil since the June assault. They were also patient, as could be noted when one of their number, long gone in drink, kept interrupting the proceedings with muttered non sequiturs. The others hushed him gently; and after a time he subsided in sleep.

Meantime Padre Antonio kept his counsel; seated to one side, he smoked and listened. His task, for a time, was done; he had chauffeured us here; we, not he, were the pupils at this school of survival.

We sat there, Gene, Dennis, and I, beyond weariness; the "night chief" dealing as best he might with our desultory questions. Indeed, we knew before we spoke that the conversation admitted of no debate. The men were there in order to repel, with all necessary force, an unjust assault on life and property; simple as that. We, the night visitors, could take it or leave.

Sleepless, seated among the bristling guns, filthy slept-in khaki, the bearded and exhausted militia, I felt curiously detached; I belonged there and did not, someone happening by, to gain some inkling of the lives and deaths of the beleaguered. . . . Everything of agreement or objection or contention was simply suspended; I carried the skull of a sleepwalker.

And thought in a curious, floating way, of similar nights in Hanoi in 1968. There, too, I stood under assault from forces of my own country. Night after night, the bombs fell to earth, a hellish drumbeat of destruction. How much had happened since, and yet how little! The night was erupting with sardonic laughter, the laughter of the gods.

My life? I was from the U.S., a curse and a blessing. I walked a continuum of self-destructive, blind violence: the air force over the northern city of Vietnam, and, fifteen years later, the contras, contemptible mercenaries of empire, menacing an obscure town at the edge of our world. One passes one's life (or what passes for a life) in such places. And who was to discover the rhyme or reason of it all?

Indeed (so dark a night, the questions even darker) was human life something more than a feeble rear-guard action of the embattled? Undoubtedly in restless snatches of sleep, the militia dreamed, like Prince Harry's striplings at Agincourt, of a far different life, peaceable tasks, that "*desarrollo humano*" which the revolution had promised. And here they were.

And here we were, in the menacing dark. Children of empire, perpetual objectors, our consciences geared to a kind of metronomic no. Once more undergoing firsthand what we had known at second hand and third, yet another disaster of witless power—*eccolo*! the chroniclers of disaster; which is to say, of our lifetime.

Alas, we said to one another, our last hope, almost a hope against hope, lay in our church; a hope that persisted even after the Vietnam years, when the church too was enlisted, bought, sold—silent. But now, as we agreed, perhaps we were embarked in a different direction; the church might even offer and hear a word of peace.

The Man in the Shadows intrigued me. It was one project to ring the city with citizen guns. It was quite another to bring the unarmed Yankees along to the fireworks. Padre Antonio, like Brer Rabbit, spoke nary a word. But I saw in his exhausted face quite another strategy than the immediate one. We were borne here, I thought, as another force, a force somewhere, at some time, to be reckoned with. The North American church. As for himself, he was in Nicaragua for a lifetime—in order, apart from his immediate mission, to say something of import to the Spanish church. (And as the Irish missioners, with telling impact, had conveyed the facts of life in Nicaragua to the church of Ireland.)

Meantime, many would die; and the prospect of invasion from the U.S., as we were frequently reminded, grows by the day. As has been shown elsewhere, a kind of sanguinary showcase, Grenada and the Falklands are of great advantage to embattled politicos.

Antonio was weaving a lifeline there in the dark. His argument, the argument of his silence, went something like this. If we three could be led to see the horrid truth of the contras, then perhaps we could persuade our church to stand with the victims, after the manner of the mothers and relatives: simply to tell the truth. Then, what a wrench might be thrown into the gears and guts of power! It was an old argument, and an honorable one. And as far as it went, it was both tested and true.

My difficulty lay in the area of tactic, its concentrations and seductions. I have a strong sense of limits, gained, I think, from Gandhi and my Buddhist friends, as well as years of exposure to domestic spirits like Merton and Day. They instruct me in this way: one works, plans, dedicates a lifetime to tasks that favor the human condition; indeed, one is enjoined to do so. But the work must fall continually under close scrutiny. The carnal ties that bind one's spirit, like a strangling umbilical, to jargon of effectiveness, media hype, goals, quotas, guaranteed results—all forms and visions and expectations of nirvana—these must be discarded, placed to one side. In favor of what the Gospel calls "the one necessary thing."

The foregoing is quite possibly a large extrapolation from an event hardly noteworthy. I include it for several reasons, having to do with both experience and present realities. The experience: our need of spiritual discipline, in a quite traditional sense; of prayer that keeps first things recognizably first, reasonably free of ego, of questionable motives, and of self-adventuring.

And equally pressing (and hardly separate from the above): the need of steadfastness in the community, so many of our sisters and brothers being in prison, even as I write; enduring separation, loneliness, the hectic lot of those shuffled about by the lethal whimsy of empire. A dark night indeed for us! No results as the world reckons, no change of heart or policy; the nuclear weapons multiply; the peasants of Central America die. And we must keep on, sustaining one another as best we might, sending a word of truth as best we can articulate it—into winds most contrary. The "single eye" commended by the Gospel! By no means is it a commending of obsessiveness; rather, a spiritual metaphor drawn from optics. There is a truth to be kept at center eye; there are lesser truths to be placed to one side, less focused, less concentrated on. And the effort required to keep the focus hard and clear, and the side truths aside, is a harsh one indeed.

Let me summon, for example, the common experience of a prisoner of conscience. There are days when the life of lockup appears in its drab and menacing outline. Life takes the guise of a very demon of despair. The demon wears a cynical mask; he peddles absurdity; he probes areas of tenderness and memory, and worsens their pain. Why this moral pretension that brought you here? Of what use is it, and to whom? The world goes its way; you accomplish nothing, unless you are pleased to call disruption of family ties, loneliness, contempt—to call these accomplishments. Indeed an argument could be pressed that your "actions" have merely deepened the public alienation, given yet another handle to the guardians of law and order. . . .

At center eye suddenly: despair, its darkness and confusion. In bad focus, or none at all (at least as persuasion and moral weight are concerned)—clarity of motive, indignation, love, the leap that overcame all objection, all fear and trembling.

At such a time, one must hear the leper's bell in the deep of one's own soul—and respond, a healer to oneself. The illness is not all of life; the healing is.

•

We toured the town with Padre Juan; we must see first-hand evidence of the contra assault. They had struck with deadly precision indeed. It was modern war at its worst, war against civilians, pure terror. The power station of the city was a mass of electronic rubble. Across the road, the sawmill and its equipment had been destroyed by shelling; it once employed some two hundred men. Further up, the coffee-drying and processing facility; likewise. And in town, the radio station had been attacked by a commando group; several young radio operators were shot, their bodies burned.

•

Dennis should have played in "I Am A Camera." Yesterday he made a delicious offer to a young man and his intended, just before they proceeded from sacristy to church for their wedding. He would photograph them and present them with the photo enlarged, if he might have their address. They were of course delighted, and posed there in the doorway, looking for all the world like old-fashioned grandparents; she shy and sloe-eyed, in her black rubber shoes and severe white gown, he with slicked back hair, in blue serge stiff as cardboard. And this morning they stand together in the crowded bishop's mass; her hair is gathered in braids like the other wives.

•

I sit like a church mouse in a dry season and take account of my world; this is what I see.

The sacristy toilet is dry as a glass eye, and stinks; and so, truth told, do I, who am obliged to ablute with a scant can of water, as I wring the neck of a slow faucet. I shrug off this mood and that malaise, from time to time taking counsel with my soul, a wagging finger at face. Are you living for the moment, all eyes and no eyes, all ears and hearing nothing? In such a world as you've landed in, consider yourself blind, deaf, and dumb. And a beggar from birth. There are truths that must be told in the body language of the dead or the yet unborn. Tell them.

•

In the cathedral, the statuary makes a communality of sorts, as though the superstars of heaven were performing an *opéra bouffe,* frozen in untamed fortissimos. Tragedy, ecstasy to the nth power. The various images of Jesus proffer a very rainbow of moods, from C to bottomed out.

In one production, he looks glum under a saffron wig (and who wouldn't, given the get-up and the human scene?). In another, head impossibly aloft, he grows lightheaded in supernal air. Francis Xavier is resplendent in a new lace minisurplice. Mary walks proud in a blue cloak, her bambino sports a bonnet like a white coal bucket.

•

Antonio proposes a meeting between ourselves and a few campesino leaders.

They sit in a circle as we enter, several are perusing newspapers or church periodicals. The scene might be thought unremarkable, if one forgot that five years previous it would have been impossible; literacy among the peasants was practically nonexistent. But now, the formerly improbable had come to pass; the campesinos looked up from their reading and greeted us, matter of factly. They were literate in other ways too, as shortly became evident.

For a starter (they questioning us): What do you think of our bishops? Talk about tendentious! There floated above the head of the questioner, like a balloon with a message, an entire world of implication. The bishops' silence, the contra assaults on the cities. The bishops' constant plaint and grievances against the government. The bishops' call for "dialogue with all parties, even those taking up arms." The bishops vis-à-vis the Jesuits, the Franciscans, Maryknollers. The bishops and the power of nostalgia, colonial longings, power, property, and *La Prensa*. The bishops, the pope, and the popular church; which is to say, the bishops and the campesinos.

And again (the tables were turned, they posed the question): Have you seen any communism in our country? Have you seen things being done for the poor? What things? They were good socratic teachers, relentless, sensing that the right question posed is itself a mode of learning, on both sides.

Then it was our turn. How has the revolution changed your lives? Their reply: Before, to be a campesino was to be abandoned, a nobody, a zero. All that is changed now. We have medical help, our children are vaccinated. Also though the contra attacks are cruel and destroy fields and crops, the government gives us food and finances, until we can make a new start. Formerly none of us could read. Now we are teaching others to read. Because everyone in Nicaragua wants to be a new person.

•

> One is struggling for life itself
>   when one struggles against death,
>   against an oppressive system.
> For when the system is anti-life
>   one chooses between life and death.

> There is no neutral ground.
> I choose to favor life
>   and struggle against death.
> This gives life to my faith.
> When I struggle at the side of my people
>   for life,
>   my faith itself comes alive.
>
> > A Campesino of Nicaragua

•

I pause in the park, near the statue of the formidable cleric who ruled the cathedral roost for two generations. He died early in the century; but his beetling mien induces, even at fifty years' remove, thoughts that could only be called chastening.

Evidently he was in command when, in 1927, U.S. Marines, five hundred strong, invaded Nicaragua to "protect American interests." Across the square from his statue stand the military barracks the marines inhabited. And on a nearby wall, a commemorative fresco of a sorry event: two small zooming biplanes; the mournful distinction commemorated: "Ocotal, the first city of Latin America to suffer aerial bombardment."

If the image is accurate, monsignor was remarkably ugly. He leans forward impatiently from his pedestal, in a kind of beefy Churchillian hunch, as though he saw human nature through a glass, darkly. In his days, which were the days of Somoza and of "American interests," we were reminded at the wrecked sawmill that a thirty-five-year-old standing tree was priced at thirty-five cents. American, Somozan interests indeed! The calculation and its implication were such that even a campesino could hold them firm: What indeed was he worth?

•

Lately, we were told, the monsignor is honored locally as a saint, to the perturbation of the bishop. One popular report has the faithful placing jars of water on his tomb, then dispensing it as blessed.

The point of such rumor is unclear to me. Perhaps it belongs under a heading like, "Local Apocrypha."

•

Said bishop, by the way, is of interest beyond the ordinary. He is regarded as one of the least reactionary of his peers. Yet he was able, during the campesino Mass, to tack with the winds, and keep the worship at a safe remove from life's chills and fevers. I was led to recall another scene, in Belfast during the hunger strike of the Long Kesh prisoners. The local pastor, Canon Murphy, refused to allow the names of prisoners to be called out during Mass. So after considerable palaver, and the canon, like the cat of the tale, being absent, the mice would have their day. Not in the church precincts surely, but in a bare community hall. The people apologized: it's already Saturday night; it's difficult to get the word about; there will be only a few of us. But the word got around, and in Canon Murphy's purloined (for the occasion) splendor, we proceeded to commemorate, of all strange and daunting events of life, a hunger strike. And, need it be added, the names of the prisoners rang out loud and clear.

•

The heartbreaking strength of people! Though we are less than three weeks distant from the ruinous attack on Ocotal, I was told of a girl who one morning attended the burial of her brother; and the same afternoon was salvaging and sacking grain, after the fires in the storage area. She and many others, invite reflection on the wellsprings of love and hope, choked by tragic event, then running free once more.

•

Alfonso takes me about the town. His English is faultless. He studied engineering at Notre Dame; since returning to Ocotal, he worked as a technician at the radio station. Then one night he saw his companions beaten, shot, and their bodies burned; he barely emerged alive, crouching behind a door during the carnage.

He pointed out the new station, which was in operation in new quarters within forty-eight hours of the assault.

The radio, he explained, is much more than a source of entertainment. It is a lifeline of the poor, who send messages of all kinds over the air, certain that relatives and friends will hear: congratulations on a birthday, a successful surgery, assurance of one's safety after a border attack.

I heard such messages being broadcast: "I have arrived safely, do not worry." "Maria has been taken to hospital, we will send news of her condition." "The following have returned unharmed, having escaped kidnapping. . . . " And then, on the part of local authorities: "Citizens, be alert and diligent, another attack is quite probable."

•

Crazy as life appears, and enigmatic and muddled and seldom easy—still, in the dusty park of a beleaguered city, I summon gratitude. Whatever first thoughts intrude, or second or third—there is no deadly sense of lost time on a lost planet. I wish with all my heart that the world were differently arranged. I wish all contras and their foreign masters were condemned to indefinite repentance and repairing of their crimes. At the same time, I feel in no way disposed to lay the burden of the world on God, an act which smacks to me of injustice toward the Just One. The longer I live, the more deeply the sinfulness of humankind afflicts; but at the same time, a corrective grace enters, like water in a desert place; I confess the saving compassion of our Lord. Saving even toward me.

Beyond doubt, I will depart this vale without having to any degree altered the lavic course of catastrophe. Alas, for all goodwill and sweat and tears, few of us could claim to mitigate, let alone prevent, the onslaught of the civilized vandals, the contras of the world. The world goes its way; and the best one can summon is a refusal, more or less steady, to go the world's way. This I realize, is no more than an epitaph, and a minor one at that.

Still, given everything, not a bad life. And at times (times like this) I can even summon a *"mucho gusto"* at the delectable prospect of the next round.

On the way back to Managua, a stop at "heroic Estelí," the title given by the revolutionary government to the town for its extraordinary resistance in the last days of Somoza.

There to meet with a minister of the Word, Rodolfo Rodríguez (who also owns and operates the Shell gas station), and José Bravo, pastor of an outlying area. The two were determined (to the point of near stupefaction on our part) to offer a detailed lecture on the history of local resistance, as it effected momentous political changes in the country at large.

We sat in the courtyard of Rodolfo's home; the rain came and went; the sun showed face and then vanished. The children, the maids, family members passed through; the ordinary routine of a day at home. Rodolfo was obviously in charge of the session, and just as obviously enjoying it; he worked a blackboard, sought out a stick of chalk, drew detailed diagrams. A born teacher; and no offense intended if the scholars, their fervor dampened by the steamy day, tended to nod betimes.

The following is a (more or less) verbatim report of the session:

> Some fifteen years ago, ten married couples began to meet with a few priests and the bishop. Questions were raised that had lain dormant for a long time, questions like: What does faith, our faith, offer the poor? We began to understand that faith required us to take the path Jesus took; and this realization led further, to many commitments.
>
> Among the first couples were the mother and father of the mayor of Ocotal; they were later kidnapped and murdered by the contras.
>
> We tried above all to be practical, to face things. Does being a Christian mean worshiping the Lady of Guadalupe, or does it mean following Jesus; and if the latter, what are the consequences? At this point some fell away from the group; others came in.
>
> In 1976 things hottened up. Asking questions, especially questions about faith, was becoming dangerous. The Somozans wanted Christians who would pray—and do nothing.
>
> Our group began to meet with a larger number of Chris-

tians in Managua, including the Cardenal brothers. It was becoming clear that the issue was survival. We must take care of those who were starving, and we must organize our self-defense. And perhaps most urgent of all, we must help others begin questioning why such conditions as we were enduring should exist at all.

By now the Sandinistas were in the hills; young folk from the university were joining them, and the first military strikes began. Sandinistas up to this point included: insurrectionists, some workers, and those who were urging a prolonged war. But there was no organizational link between them and our Christian groups.

In 1966 and 1967, the war began in earnest. So we Christians began to organize our structure of self-defense, house by house, in this whole region. There were only a handful of us, to start. On each block five people were elected as "responsibles." They were put in charge of the following: organization, health, food, defense, and coordination. All those in charge were Christians. Four blocks constituted a "zone." And as the areas increased, more people were included through elections and delegated authority. By then, the killing was widespread. We were forced to work quickly.

Only through tight organization, we realized, could we confront the guardia with any hope of success; they were, by now, simply on rampage. If one member disappeared (and many did), another would quickly take his or her place. Potential spies were discouraged. The coordinators had to know who was weak, who might even be a secret member of the guardia, as well as those who could be depended on.

Each house had an escape route. If a meeting were being held within and the guardia appeared in their jeeps, word went around on the instant, and the whole neighborhood poured out and surrounded them. And if they demanded that someone be produced, everyone shouted out: "I'm the one! Take me!" It was completely demoralizing for them.

We also developed a strategy of warning. We had to know who came and went in the neighborhood, and for what reason. So we developed different signals. We used drums, pots, pans, a different beat, different signals. Thus no one was taken unawares, and the guardia found it more and more difficult to make inroads on us.

Up to then, we were one group, the Sandinistas another. Each of us had our own purpose and methods; we hardly knew one another. It was the Christians who did the basic organizing in our area; not many Sandinistas were about.

Other groups arose, inevitably; the Somozans were so greedy they began seizing property even from the wealthy; that's always dangerous! So the rich families turned to the workers and said, "If you'll go on strike, we'll guarantee your wages!"

Then the political parties came round, began to join the resistance. They called on our base communities to join them. We said, "Not for your interests alone; it was we who had inspired and led the first strikes." The FSLN began to understand that in unity our only hope lay; each group must stand with the other, or we all disappear.

The part the church played was crucial. It was the church that had access to all classes, and could move with a measure of freedom among all. The church was trusted; it could also criticize what went on, no matter where. So it was respected; everyone acknowledged that the church was playing an indispensable part in the resistance. It was not just the "religious arm" of the Sandinistas.

In the base communities, the sisters and priests were active from the first. Much of the responsibility for health needs was taken by the nuns. Priests were near the top echelons of the organizations, but secretly, under threat of death as many of them were. In town here for instance, there were two churches where people could be protected and hidden. This became known to the guardia, and one church was later bombed by Somoza.

As far as the bishops were concerned, they took no part in these events. We concluded they didn't know much, because they didn't want to know. They also had rich connections, and this tended to retard them. Only late in the game did the bishops condemn the violence of all sides. In a clever stroke, the front enlisted Archbishop Obando, in a sense forced his hand. They asked him to act as intermediary when they took hostages. This gave him prestige, and gave them leverage; they could now show, before the world, their respect for ecclesiastics. But the priests were something else; they were united around our work, and the people trusted them.

In 1978, the bishop of Estelí died, and for a long time no successor was appointed. That was all right with us; we had a saying: no bishop, no problem.

In September of that year, there was an insurrection in the city. Twenty-one Sandinistas came in secretly from the mountains, and the people organized around them. The guardia was strong and vicious, one thousand in number. The U.S. supplied them with bombers and ammunition. But in spite of the cruel bombardment, the people won out; they massacred the guardia, for sixty-three days; only a few managed to hide out and eventually escape. Then we began reconstruction; the town was in rubble. We built about five hundred homes that year, and thousands since.

You recall that in 1979 our bishops issued a pastoral letter strongly supporting the revolution. A great contrast to their recent one! But our people understand the influence of wealth on the bishops and their support of Somoza. We have had to learn to be independent of bishops. We say, well, they just don't understand. . . . In consequence, people don't break with the church, any more than we abandon our political convictions, just because the church objects.

•

Back to Managua, a pleasant, innocuous hour with Ernesto Cardenal. He occupies a second-storey office, in what had once been an immense hacienda of Somoza, a holding so vast it was quite impossible from the main house, to spot the outside wall of the property.

We laughingly recalled that poor assailed Nicaragua has appointed a Minister of Culture, while the U.S. boasts no such appointment. We ventured moreover that were such an office to be created in Washington, the incumbent might occupy a broom closet off a shabby back corridor (in the Pentagon, perhaps!) and be instructed to install, among other delights, a series of Tiffany windows portraying sainted generals and admirals, their countenances haloed in nuclear glare! (Cultural note: such windows are already installed there.)

We brought up the subject of the former proprietor of the estate, and the irony of Ernesto's presence on such premises. He smiled. "There must be many ghosts walking these stairs," I said. "But we never think of it now as Somoza's house," he answered. "Only as the Ministry of Culture." He, like almost everyone here, predicts harder days ahead for Nicaragua if Reagan is reelected, an outcome which, we assured him, was a strong probability.

All the public officials, as well as the Jesuits, are haunted by this. They speak with sorrow of the economic hardships resulting from the indiscriminate attacks of the contras. Some even believe a direct invasion of Nicaragua would be unnecessary, since the economic destruction could well make the country ungovernable. Few seem to think that European aid will carry them through.

•

Laid low once more, this time mercifully for a day only. Montezuma's ghost at large.

When asked to describe my plight, I reply with infinite delicacy that were I to open my jaws like a python, one might well see daylight at the other end. . . .

•

César Jerez, near legend in the Jesuits, former superior of Central America, expert in many trades, agile apologist for the brethren, scholar—if I sound for all the world like an old-fashioned hagiographer, so be it!

(When Jerez lectured at a Jesuit college in the U.S. a year ago, reaction on campus included such remarks, from fellow Jesuits, as: "We wonder at times whether the brethren of Central America are more devoted to Marxism than to Christianity. . . .")

In any case, Jerez came across town from the university to spend a few hours with us. On every subject his mind touched on (a mind like a lantern of fireflies) he surprised and illumined. He spoke about the Jesuits and about the conflicts in the church of Nicaragua:

> The bishops describe our situation in the only terms they know, as a kind of "vertical problem." This is inaccurate. The "popular church," if you regard the phenomenon across Latin America, includes all strata of authority and sacrament; there are cardinals, bishops, priests, and lay people, all of whom identify with this or that community. To limit the development, as is done here, to priests and laity, is simply to falsify it. It is certainly true that the Nicaraguan bishops have placed themselves in opposition to our base communities; but this attitude is due to circumstances peculiar to Nicaragua; above all, the heavy influence of the Somoza years is still with us in the bishops whose appointment the old guard once approved. . . .
>
> There is hope that with the election of a new general of our order, things in Rome may calm down; at least one may hope so. I once said to [former Superior General] Arrupe: "You must do more lobbying, both with the pope and the chief cardinals." He said simply: "This is not my style; I have no talent for this." Yet we know how nearly the pope came to intervening and appointing a cardinal head of the order. . . .
>
> At that crucial time, the cardinal of Guatemala said to me sternly: "We are going to have to suppress you Jesuits all over again." And I replied: "That will take some doing; why don't you start the process?"
>
> Everywhere in the church, the bishops' dilemmas revolve almost entirely around third world issues and situations. This is extremely instructive. It raises the question, in regard to us Jesuits: Are we merely to be in service to the poor, or are we to be ourselves poor?

•

In 1980 a congress was organized with the support of Pinochet of Chile, Stroessner of Paraguay, and the army officers of Uruguay. Its subject was purportedly anticommunism. But the real purpose seems to have been a proposal: the expulsion of all Jesuits from Latin America [IFOR report, Holland].

> If these people
> are so worried about us,
> it means that we are doing something right.
> I see the Jesuit aspiration
> as the service of faith through justice.
> The trouble is
> that promoting justice
> implies consequences.
> If we take this task seriously
> and join it to the tenets of the Bible,
> it could take the life of each of us.
> I say this with all tranquility;
> this is not the same as suicide.
> But the gospel is very clear:
> speaking up for the kingdom of Jesus—
> the kindom of love, justice, truth, freedom,
> peace—in our circumstance
> this means offering one's life.
>
> Luis Pérez Aguirre, S.J.

•

Jerez again: "One of the worst mistakes we can make is, for whatever reason, to turn to the right, thus becoming a force in the suppression of the left. If we do this, we deny a future for the order. On the other hand, Archbishop López Trujillo has said with obvious implications that one of the last tricks of the left, was to introduce class struggle into the church." (No comment, or almost none, except for this query: When has class conflict ever been absent from the church? See, for example, the diatribe [ca. A.D. 35-45] in the Letter of James: "For if a man with gold rings and in fine clothing comes into your assembly, and a poor man in shabby clothing also comes in, and you pay attention to the one who wears the fine clothing . . . " [James 2:2-7].)

Jerez: "Historically, the orders have prevented the church

from being torn up into dissident sects, as the pope was forced to take into account new gifts of the Spirit, erupting unexpectedly here and there. In such ways, new gifts and directions and forms broadened the central understanding, increased the areas of necessary freedom. But the current word from headquarters is something else: 'You come to us and be told what to do!' "

•

The motto of our *la strada* trio: "magic, mummery, make do." The good humor and patience of Gene and Dennis make the trip more than bearable, a joy.

Yesterday we spent hours in the burning sunshine, trying to hail a cab. The buses, given my spinal condition, are out of the question. And the cabs are rare as hen's teeth; those that are limping along are crowded to the gunwales, and pass one by, huffing like overloaded pachyderms. More stranded people, less and less public transport as parts give out, and no replacements arrive. It's called embargo, a U.S. specialty.

•

Three years ago, I hung Romero's photo on the wall at home; and I wondered what it must be like, that those you work with die as martyrs. . . .

Then last night at table, Jerez, pointing to the images on the wall: "Romero and I were friends; he was an intelligent and holy man. . . . " He pointed to another image: "He succeeded me at such and such a job, and they killed him." And another: "He was murdered in Guatemala a few years ago." Dennis reflected afterward: "If in the States we had such examples to draw on, wouldn't we have a deeper love of the Society, and couldn't we use a word like 'charism' more truthfully?" (He knows how I detest the word, cheaply tossed about as it is, both cover and claim.)

•

> I greatly fear that very soon
> the gospel will not be allowed
> within our country.

Only the bindings will arrive, nothing else—
    because all the pages are subversive.
And if Jesus were to cross the border
    they would arrest him.
They would take him to many courts
    and accuse him of being subversive, unconstitutional,
    a revolutionary, a foreign Jew,
    a concocter of strange, bizarre ideas.
They would crucify him again
    because they prefer a Christ
    of sacristy or cemetery
    a silent Christ
    a Christ according to our image
    and our selfish interests.

Rutilio Grande, S.J.

•

Compounded absurdity and danger. The government has announced that a priest of the diocese has been taken, *flagrante delicto,* in process of storing arms, with a view toward sabotage. They promptly delivered him to the papal nuncio, a curious decision, in the nature of a throwback to an old colonial arrangement. The nuncio, of course, informed the archbishop, who sounded the tocsin of alarm: "this being another effort of the government to discredit the church. . . . "

On television last night the government showed videotapes of said priest, the tapes purporting to show him conspiring with others, discussing crimes in preparation, disposition of aforesaid lethal goodies, etc. It is all very sad, and given the church-state imbroglio, quite predictable. When I inquired as to particulars of the accused cleric, one of the Jesuits said offhandedly: "Oh, he's the one who yells epithets at us when we attend meetings of the priests, is always demanding expressions of loyalty to the Holy Father. . . . "

We discussed events that evening. One of the Jesuits: "A difficulty is that the junta hasn't learned the difference between being an opposition group and a government. They were in the hills too long, a minority too long. . . . "

How then should they have dealt with the priest?

"They should simply have announced that he would be tried according to the law, like anyone else. But as things stand, he'll be freed by the nuncio and returned to his parish by the bishop, who will thereupon organize public demonstrations against the 'atheistic Marxist government and its persecution of the church.' "

Which is exactly what happened. (Followed by yet another gaffe of the authorities. They expelled from the country a number of priests who had taken part in the demonstrations. Thereby half-wittedly [it could hardly have been unwitting, if one concedes a measure of savvy to the government] inviting righteous alarm both in Washington and Rome.)

•

A strange intermingling of sacred and military symbols (shades of the IRA in northern Ireland!):

Signs and silhouettes in public places: *"SANDINO VIVE!"* A quasi-Christ figure, a kind of invocation of resurrection.

Mottoes abound: "PATRIA LIBRE O MORIR!"

Downtown, enormous portraits of the heroes of the resistance still in place: the backdrop of the platform from which the pope launched his fateful, fretful homily to the massed crowds.

Someone showed me the embolism of the Lord's Prayer composed for that day:

> Our Father who dwells with us in our land of
> > Nicaragua,
> > blessed be your name
> > in our untiring search for justice and peace.
> Your kingdom come
> > for those who have waited so long
> > for a life of dignity.
> Your will be done on earth as in heaven
> > and in the church of Nicaragua,
> > a church on the side of the poor.
> Give us this day our daily bread
> > that we may build a new society.

Forgive us our offenses.
And lead us not into the temptation
 of believing that we are already
 new women and men.
And deliver us from the evil of war
 and the evil of forgetting that our lives
 and the life of Nicaragua are in your hands.
Amen.

•

Burdened as we temporary expatriates are with the sights and sounds and stories of "contra country" (evidence as well of the crimes of our political leaders in the U.S.), this one is tempted to yield to fatalism, a frigid numbing of spirit. How desperately easy to whisper to one's spirit: Violence is again carving its swath through history; indeed, is itself creating history. The contras and their imperial masters know the game so well, and its rules, a game loaded from the start. What good sense it would make simply to throw in the sponge. . . . Then with what effort, one exorcises this diseased "analysis of the embassy."

Let me confess it: I don't understand much that goes on here chez les Jésuites. The nuances of a conversation often escape me; I'm here for too short a time; the language proceeds at normal (which is to say breakneck) pace. . . . It's common knowledge, for instance, that a few of the Jesuits have been under Roman scrutiny for some time for their connections with the junta. One has the impression of a tightly knit community following its own lights, and no resolution of conflict in sight.

I suggested to Jerez: "Even if the tensions between the Jesuits and the bishops in Guatemala or Salvador or Nicaragua were resolved tomorrow, important questions would undoubtedly remain. For example, the relationship to be adopted between the church and government, whether revolutionary or repressive. No?" He agreed.

They look for helpful developments between the Jesuits here and those in North America. Dennis and I hope to have part in such on our return.

•

There is a look on the faces of the military in Salvador that can only be described as feral. This is true of those especially who guard the banks and the homes of the wealthy. One has a sense in their presence that literally anything could happen at any moment. This being commonly assumed, people tend to take the long way round such characters.

In Nicaragua, soldiers armed with machine guns patrol the streets; and no one turns a hair. Soldiers elbow into the crowded buses, holding their impeding sten guns overhead; they are simply part of a good-natured, if groaning, crowd. Yesterday on the grounds of the Ministry of Culture, I saw a soldier making the rounds between buildings. He was armed with—rolls of toilet paper! Said to Dennis: "Would that every soldier in the U.S. were thus usefully employed!"

And this morning when our trio shoehorned into an already overcrowded cab, I found myself doing a siamese twin act with an armed soldier; his gun was pressing as tightly against my thigh as against his own, a taste of involuntary armament or forced induction or something. In any case, the soldier evinced considerable curiosity regarding our non-Nicaraguan phizes. Where were we from? No trace of resentment was evident at our answer; we might have been Patagonians or Upper Voltaians. And the warmest of conversations got underway, as though friendship were some sort of instant mix, and we the imbibers.

•

This noon we wandered through the immense central market and ate well and cheaply there. Loaded food stands adjoining one another in friendly olefactory contest, signs announcing various ultimates and superlatives: "Rosita's cooking, known for quality." Or urging the throngs: "Try María Menendez, who takes good care of her clients." A market vivid in color and varied in scope, A to Z; farm products, handicrafts, foods and drinks, bolts of cloth and finished clothing, all displayed in big open sheds, architecturally quite attractive.

•

Thumbing through the history books, one gains a vivid sense of the suffering that marks the past decade here. (To limit the fact of suffering to that period is arbitrary of course. "American interests" have invaded, captured, repressed, raped, for three generations.) A sense as well of the enormous patience and goodness of the people. To survive, to have one's family survive, not to be plunged in mourning for the murder of a close relative—an enormous boon, which in fact only a few families achieve. Sweetness of spirit, the persistence of life.

•

The school question simmers away, we were told. The government is urging the teaching of Marxist analysis of history and economics, among other theories. But the bishops claim the government is bent on destroying the faith of the young.

The atmosphere is poisoned. It results in spasms of reaction, which might be considered outrageously funny if they were not so deadly vindictive. Like the rush to defend priests, under whatever murky circumstance (including the worthy arrested for insurrectionary tendencies). Or the arbitrary expulsion of priests and nuns, darkly (and foolishly) reminiscent of other, utterly unlike regimes elsewhere.

•

The Christians of Jalapa, the northern city long assaulted by the contras, issued a "reflection paper" at Easter time. It was designed for use by the base communities; its occasion was the issuing, shortly before, of the bishops' pastoral letter on reconciliation.

I found the reflections remarkable on many counts, translated it as best I could, and append it here, in summary fashion:

There are in our midst signs of the Kingdom of God, and signs of the reign of darkness.

Among the first: The lands that have been distributed among the campesinos, an act which makes real the promise of Christ that the meek will inherit the land. Then, the cooperatives, in which peasants share equally in the means of production, and thus verify the equality of the children of God. Also, the building of homes for the displaced poor; and the vaccinations, which in our area 98 percent of the people have received; this seems to us to corroborate the promise of Christ that we shall have life, and have it more abundantly. Also, the national amnesty, helping toward reconciliation with those who repent their errors. Further, we pay tribute to the courage of the workers and peasants, who produce food and the necessities of life in the face of aggression. Through them, the people exercise and direct the life God has given us.

Let us also rejoice in the life of our Christian communities, who give "reason for the faith that is in us." With humility we state our firm intention to follow and witness to the Christ who announces good news to the poor, welcomes the children, and expels the merchants from the temple; this Christ who gave his life and is risen from the dead is become Lord of life.

•

> In all our Latin American countries
> the church. . .would be mutilating the gospel
> if we reduced it, as some would like,
> to just talking
> about spirituality and family problems—
> as if truths revealed by God
> would not also illuminate
> economic, social, and political reality.
>
> Bishops of Guatemala

•

And then in the reflection paper from Jalapa I find this "sign," over which I stumble mightily: "Finally, we salute our brothers in the battalions, in the patriotic military service, in the frontier guard, etc. These brothers edify us by their lives, even to the giving of their lives on behalf of all."

Evidently, the reference here is to the Gospel passage: "This is my commandment, that you love one another as I have loved you" (John 15:12).

But I find the commentary treacherously thin, an example of the ease with which scripture is tossed about—in this case to justify war. And I think of Ellul's statement: "for fifteen hundred years, we have had just wars of the right; now in our century, we are asked to accept just wars of the left. . . . "

•

In such times, what are we to make of the command to love even our enemies, to do good to those who persecute and demean us, to turn the other cheek? Whether in Nicaragua or in mainline theology of the U.S. or Europe, such texts are not commonly invoked. There is undeniably a high ideal in such words, we are told, but little of practical value, since (as everyone knows) there exists no conscience on the other side, the enemy is not to be trusted, etc.

The best we can make of the situation, according to one renowned divine, is to construct something he calls an "interim ethic," which seems to mean, as far as one can tell, that we continue to explore, in practice and theory, the boundaries of allowable murder. This (until such time as the Lord's return will make all things right) being the acceptable mode of promulgating apodictically, and once for all, the famous Sermon on the Mount of Divine Frustration.

A sermon which the course of history, including Christian history, has chosen with wondrous consistency severally to ignore or learnedly debase or refashion to dark uses.

•

If any measure of wisdom may be said to arrive with age and experience, it takes the form of distrust and skepticism—first of all of the virtue of one's own conduct; then of one's generation as well. The opposing presumption being that somehow or other those now alive have managed (somehow or other) to stand outside history. And are therefore in the advantageous position of improving upon all that went before. We are "come of age" as it were. But what that "age" might be, if touted up, not in years but in moral accountability—we are somewhat less than skilled at this, somewhat less than enthused. We prefer to leave such a project to the victims and martyrs "crying out from beneath the altar"—the judges of each and all, according to scripture. The ones who, having given their lives for others, stand outside our bloody communal history. The only ones, in consequence, who could claim with any logic to have "come of age. . . . " And about whose gift to us and others we are not ordinarily inclined to inquire, even at worship.

•

Granted the worst of time and the horror from which Nicaraguans have emerged, one still regrets that certain questions are not being raised. We have yet to hear, from the Jesuits or anyone else, a serious discussion of the Beatitudes, for instance. A fact which seems all the more strange since the text of the liturgy we celebrated last night was precisely Matthew 5!

Again, the Jalapa text, which seemed to me, when I first took it up, not far short of miraculous—it founders on the same haunting questions we must constantly face at home: Are Christians allowed to kill or approve of or be complicit in killing?

•

Complexities abound. They remind me of the detritus left on shore when a tide recedes.

If one can read the evidence, picking up and examining this or that, the motionless crustaceans, the dead shells, the text of whorl and curve and stain—what an open sesame to our past! We are in fact holding up a mirror; the face we see is our own.

•

A Jesuit reported that we could expect the bishops shortly to announce their opposition to universal military service. He gave the news dispiritedly. And I was silent, whether from plain cowardice or clumsy Spanish or an overfastidious sense of being a guest in the house. But the dilemma was no less clear for being implied; the Jesuits support military service as a necessity of political survival. While the bishops (for what could only be called the worst of reasons) object to the same development.

The right thing for the wrong reason, the wrong thing for the right reason . . . it is hardly a nursery jingle that runs and runs in the mind; more like the choral ode of a Sophoclean tragedy.

But the dilemma forces a question and an answer and sheds a light of its own, and not only on Jesuits or bishops. Violence for just (or unjust) causes? We need ask where indeed Christians, in Nicaragua, the U.S., or anywhere, stand (stand and refuse to move) on this question, which is the question of our lifetime—a question recalcitrant, thrice knotted, tightly drawn, a very noose about our neck; the double strand of injustice and war.

The question rose up mightily in Nicaragua, and we from the U.S. could hardly wash our hands of it; the stain of blood lay on us also; hands that handed over the guns, the bombers, the savvy. . . .

•

A long procession of children passes by, granted a holiday in honor of the birthday of Carlos Fonseca, greatest hero of the revolution. There are children in pseudograss skirts of plastic, others in homemade masks. A pregnant woman goes by with her little son. She walks laboriously, but with grace, like a galleon sailing along in the wind. No birth control here! Across the street, a filthy yard; trucks parked, leaking oil and stench. Then a three-sided shed, a rickety shelter. In it, a child is rocking an infant in a hammock.

And a host of impressions crowd in on me: Nicaragua, explosive with art in every direction, chockablock with life. The posters reenact the Passion of Christ with modern figures—crucified campesinos, mothers of the disappeared miming Mary's dolors, a naked child under a vatic star, the U.S. in the inevitable role of wicked Herod.

A clumsy recognition scene, north and south. For years, in the peace movement, in civil rights' days, we drew on the same biblical imagery, in street theatre, leaflets, days of retreat. Truly, in Central America, as at home, the Gospel is cut to the bone. And the bones, clumsy as articulated sticks, walk abroad! A danger here: to take sides, draw lines, so that the Gospel becomes a superior military handbook (nonviolent of course, on our side of course!).

•

One can even come to believe that for the "enemy" death is the only redemption. Such sinister fantasies sometimes wear a religious guise, the worst and darkest of them become a matter of God's will. (Thus Mr. Reagan reportedly, during a voice-over practice prior to a radio speech, intoned something like: "I have just declared Russia obsolete; the bombing will start in five minutes." And Mr. Reagan is a virtuous man.)

Jesus was, to say the least, slightly less certain about what are called human certainties. I am helped by noting that his fiercest language is reserved for hypocrites in high places, invariably, to be sure, with a view to conversion and reconciling.

Right action, wrong reason . . . the old refrain. I believe, along with the Nicaraguan bishops, in "dialogue with all parties, including those who have taken up arms." But if one is to commend reconciliation, so much depends on one's own moral geography! Suppose, for instance, that there were evident in the bishops the clarity and courage of a Romero. (Suppose it of us all.) Suppose further that the bishops were dispossessed, even victimized and threatened, as are the Maryknollers and Jesuits (and most grievously of all, as are the campesinos whom their excellencies so urgently homilize).

This, I suggest, is the indispensable prelude to any commendation of virtuous action: that one first perform the acts commended. More: the truthfulness of one's life verifies the biblical truth (which, one presumes, underlies the bishops' call), namely, as previously suggested, that Christ has reconciled us, one to another. In consequence, there remains the task of renouncing our dark infidelities, in all their forms, in favor of welcoming the sublime *opus operatum,* the act once and for all done—without us, even in spite of us. I am constantly reminded: one must tread softly here. To be taken in account with utmost seriousness is the actuality of Nicaragua—a first generation of survivors, very sons (and daughters) of thunder. Survivors who have known murder and pillage and torture, right hand and left. And have emerged in the main, wonderfully unscarred, renouncing revenge, determined on the works of social justice.

No mere theorizing will do. Moral geography is all; or nearly so, if truth is the object.

I wonder if such matters are discussed in base communities. I wonder if second thoughts arise, which would cast a certain hesitant doubt on the conferring of a blessing, the blessing of Christ, on violence. I wonder if the church is raising such doubts, questions, evoking such second (and third) thoughts.

•

> In the parish of Santa María de los Angeles outside
>   Managua the saint figures have been removed
> In their place are murals
>   that glorify the Sandinista Revolution
>   including pictures of two revolutionary heroes . . .
> Carlos Fonseca and Augusto Sandino.
>
> Behind the altar
>   the unfinished portrait
>   of a man with arms outstretched
>   towers above the sanctuary.
> He is the "new man,"
>   the man the liberation theologians
>   and Sandinista government
>   are now bent on creating.
>
> Chris Hedges

•

Meantime, at home the role of religious peace people remains a humiliated one, if we truly grasp it. We have much to learn, and for Dennis and myself much to absorb and bring back.

Among the questions: Can we discern the signs of Easter and Pentecost in our own communities (can we create such signs? are our lives such signs?) as do these peasants with such eloquent faith? The question seems to me to be reduced to a formula which is both cruel and exact: to the degree in which death tests the spirit and substance of our lives, to that degree the signs are created and clarified. (But I know too that death can further obscure the signs.)

Also to be noted: in comparison with matters like liberation theology, base communities, etc., our forms and efforts have little world currency. For many reasons. The theology we write (and try to live) is little known elsewhere. This, is due either to the cowardice and laziness of publishers or to a point of view, implicit throughout Latin America, that little of value can come out of an imperial culture—or its church.

Also, few if any North American theologians could be called "theologians of peace" in any sense comparable to the "theologians of liberation." Indeed the interests of mainline theologians in the U.S. go in totally other directions (always excepting the admirable and crusty John McKenzie). So saying, I indulge in a massive and charitable understatement: one of the most courageous of the peace bishops recently remarked to me that "your Jesuit theologians not only have not supported our pastoral letter, they have publicly objected and opposed us." Enough said.

•

A child sleeps in its hammock in the shed. Now the young mother takes up an ax, starts splitting wood in the torrid noon. The sun strikes off her blade. The wood makes a fire that makes the noon meal. It is all simple and primitive and direct, as though some new beginning of things were being underscored in an exhausted and depleted world. Another sense of time, another sense of reality.

•

Someone said, in the course of the inevitable discussion on the U.S. and the contras: "Mr. Reagan does not know us. [It was very like the tone and language of the Vietnamese in 1968.] We are used to being poor. We will eat the earth before we surrender our revolution."

•

The gift of these days, a slightly less clouded understanding of my place, work, ethos, discipline on return.

Somewhat like the changes rung in the course of my exodus from the U.S. in 1965, when I was shot south in a one-way rocket to Latin America. In the mellow light of memory, it appears that during the lonely continental trek, I rid myself, as though by unwelcome emetic, of a measure of cultural and spiritual poison. Something like this: I changed from a "somebody" in a false sense to a "nobody" in a true sense. I became someone other than a stranger or an enemy of death, in all its guises and disguises.

I learned something at that time from people very like those I move among here; and in spite of all feints and shifts and ploys, I have been unable to unlearn it. Namely. To walk with death as another phase of walking with life. Live with it or walk away from it. I mean what I once wrote in the diary of those months: "They Call Us Dead Men." Then connections broke down in the welter of the sixties. I lost my meagre Spanish, concluded I would never return to Latin America.

And here I am. A little like Merton, in wonderment as to why I still occupy the earth in (God help us) the Reagan eighties. Surreal. Merton wrote me shortly before his death of his sense of wobbling about on a pivot, automatically writing books for reasons that made sense only to others. And I at sixty-three, remotely in command of sense and function, come to Nicaragua, where to die young and violently is a very badge of honor, a very ticket to immortality. As witness today's parades and ceremonies.

•

Something is undoubtedly awry. I have no sense of "growing old," no conception of what the phrase might mean, except as weird incantation, or a declaration by the gimlet-eyed culture that one is no longer a unit of production. Granted a minatory creak or two, I am left only with a sense that something foolish is being pushed at me, something known as "aging." As undoubtedly the same dubious theory and its consumer consolations (annuities, retirement colonies) were pushed at (and evoked the gentle derision of) Dorothy Day, Tony Walsh, A.J. Muste. This when all the while the clock of the soul, mysterious and infallible as the clock of all living things, whispers only of deeper depths and another season. . . .

•

Stalemated on the street, we wait and wait some more. *Eccolo!* We are turning slowly into very Ikons of Patience. The sun beats us into shape, a hammer of bronze. Another hour and we shall be carted off to be exhibited in some church or square: Patience On A Monument.

•

Meantime. Will there occur the promised meeting with folk of the base communities? Are we to be present? No one seems to know; the parade of children is long gone. . . .

•

Just opposite us, the palace of the papal nuncio: splendiferous, gutted, a Somozan relic. A former palace. A palace (literally); former (literally). And on its walls Signs of the Times are scrawled, an obituary:

VIVAN LAS MILICIAS POPULARES

VIGILANCIA REVOLUCIONARIA + M.P.S. =
EL PODER POPULAR

SIC TRANSIT.

•

Waiting. Dennis, for all his goodness, frets under the enforced necessity—nothing to do, doing nothing. I ask him maliciously, "Aren't you used by now to waiting outside the doors of superiors, they being invariably busied with someone or something of vastly more import than you?"

•

Thanksgiving, a very paean of it for this voyage: its friendships, high points and low, its heartstopping sights and stories. . . .

The Jesuits alone made it all worthwhile. Then, a bonus, encountering the new breed of missioners, smiling in the teeth of terror. Then the good sense of those who helped with their urging: "Don't hang around the cities; it's only the campesinos who know the realities. . . ." A statement which, time and again, was proven true, even as we swayed about in the dromedarian buses and foolishly tried out the local foods (and paid dearly for it; pale horse, pale rider).

•

It occurs also to me: one were well advised to undergo hard times at home before venturing into Nicaragua. Otherwise, no recognition scenes, only the appalling sense of being violently uprooted and set down, one knows not quite where. . . .

•

In the school of holy angels, the children are taught
    to live in this world for the sake of the next.
It is less clear that they are taught to live in this world for the
    sake of the sisters and brothers of this world.
To live in this world for the sake of others, it seems, is the
    way of Jesus; through his way we live for the
    next world.
This is a subtle art, too clearly taught us to be easily avoided;
    though for a long time measures of avoidance
    have been taught.

•

Psychomedical note on being this age and still on my feet. Clues: loving family members who stand at my side and I at theirs. A community of friends (to whom I want in the future to make a better contribution). Finally (a sublime final cause), faith in Christ, which has proven neither illusion nor front nor bribe.

•

Our time is winding down; we've met with practically everyone accessible. Dennis and Gene find the still waters hard to tread; they feel becalmed. Dennis avers he doesn't mind waiting interminably here and there; he just doesn't want to wait "without purpose!"

I, on the other hand, never having had a purpose worth spit—to me, the waiting is a fine thing, almost a vocation.

My secret is freely given: open a third eye on this third world; close the other two!

Meantime, while I revel in the spinning of airy thought, it is Gene who lines up at the crowded street phones, does the dog work. All praise to him.

•

An end of hanging about. Thanks to John of Maryknoll and his serviceable Land Rover, we lurch along a rocky barrio road. And arrive at a Jesuit outpost and a Padre Fernando, a Spaniard in Nicaragua for some thirty years. While we took coffee, a mad tropical rainfall drummed multivocally on the tin roof. The usual photos on the wall: Sister Maura, the murdered nun, had worked in this area. Fernando said: "I told her when she left for Salvador, 'You are going to your death.' But she shook her head with that smile of hers that could break your heart and said, 'It is not so.' She was invariably smiling, except when she was at the wheel of a truck. Then she became very determined, and looked neither to right nor left."

We drove Fernando further into the barrio, to a little shanty where he was to celebrate Mass. . . .

If I need to have my faith confirmed, and indeed I do, it happens through such gracious episodes. We saw a neighborhood where only a week ago a tempest had swept away more than forty houses and all their meager chattels. Now the dispossessed dwell in tents, pitched in place of the homes. The pen chills at such tragedies.

We came on the little children's park named for the murdered nun. "Parque Maura," the rough signboard read. Children high and low in the swings, grass and flowers and Maura's smile and Rutilio Grande and the others.

•

> One steel beam
> is joined to another—
> the bridge is complete!
>
> The river below
> doesn't change,
> but the river banks
> aren't islands anymore.
>
> If I can be
> but a small beam
> to help build Chile,
>
> Then let me live
> until the banks
> aren't islands anymore!
>
> Sister Carol Piette
> + **1979**

•

The rain falls and falls, the crowds stand waiting—for buses or taxis or trucks or pickups of any sort. Less transport, more waiting, war, attrition, the throttling of the works of peace in the mailed fist. References broadside to the "yankee imperialists";

but never, on personal meeting with anyone, any tone of recrimination. I said, "It reminds me so much of Hanoi in 1968 when Zinn and I walked freely about Hanoi." I asked then, in a kind of wonderment: "How do you think the people of North Vietnam would fare these days were they walking the streets of New York?" It would require no vivid imagination to answer that one. Our bitterest enemies, in our eyes, being our own victims.

•

Yesterday someone claiming to be a Jesuit from Rome showed up at the door. His response to casually placed questions was confused, to say the least. With grandiloquence he assured the assembled brethren that, among other blessings, the Holy Father would shortly "embrace Nicaragua." This was, as the saying goes, a bit much. He was eased out the door.

•

At departure time the airport scene is immensely engaging. Officials try with all their might and main to be official; we are passed through a series of obstacles, investigations, shuffling of credentials; we are admitted, with gravity if not severity, from one to the next. Finally, the lucky seat holders, relieved of immense mounds of baggage (including dismembered Nicaraguan rocking chairs, the pieces taped together), are admitted into the final-stage waiting room.

We are now, of course, entirely bereft of accompanying families or friends, long since ejected into outer darkness, so to speak. There is a message to be conveyed, underscored even, by Latin body language and gesture: If certain people have the bad taste to leave their country, then so be it! But a price must be exacted, official approval cannot by any means be manifest. . . . (This is of course mostly malarkey. An international stereotype, something like "security considerations," determines the rubrics here.)

Still, there is an inescapable and delightful Latin tone to the goings on. The ejected family members, the nonvoyagers, evidently seek from the outside (or already are familiar with) the location of our involuntary confinement. They plant themselves outside the window; one can hear, through the massive closed drapes that separate sheep from goats, the great knocking at the windows, a clamor of Spanish desire. Those within are ready; without interference (the law is hardly the law; it is merely a decor, a sublime dodge) those in the room push aside the drapes, and lo! yin and yang, the included and the rejected, lions and lambs even—the Anglo-Saxon dictum (the law is the law is the law) is lifted once and for all. The kingdom is come; or at least part way.

The families are lip-reading through the glass; it is something like a prison visiting room. Many are sitting on the floor, just as in their own home. Here and there, a woman or child is in tears. No one arrives to object or interfere with a scene that in New York would be quite unheard of. Uniforms come and go, look and do not see. One can read the quintessential Latin lògic: 1) The curtains are thick, the windows thicker. Therefore the law is vindicated which says: no communication is allowed between travelers, once put through the needle's eye, and outsiders, 2) the curtain and window obstacle is meaningless after all. It is also demeaning, to both sides. Therefore let the human prevail!

•

As to the art of diary keeping, since this one is winding down.

Merton explained to me that he resolved, so to speak, to keep two sets of books, not one. Somewhat in the manner of the entrepreneur commended in the Gospel. One, according to the monk, was destined for the public eye: a traveler's Baedeker, a map of life within and without. The second, more chancy and altogether private, a closely guarded report, relative to the hot or icy temperature of soul; a temperature which, he judged, time would cool down.

As far as I've given time to the matter, I prefer, while paying a nod to an expedient dualism, to mix the two—a subtle cocktail of spirit.

•

Here I am in an airport, a launching pad into the, alas, all too well known. A rare moment: as though the faces of the past weeks, the lovers and malingerers, the gentle folk and the hit men, the Cherokees and churches, and then those words, words, words, wise and frivolous, momentous and self-serving, remembered and best forgotten—as though all were justified, honored, valued, judged in mercy. In Christ, that wondrous dovetailing. . . .

A sense that everything of faith, everything that beckoned me to Central America, was blessed, true, and valuable.

A sense that all will be well. That the healing of confusion, terror, and second-guessing were already underway, in spite of all. That the "in spite of," actual as it is in my life, is taken in account (as well as held accountable).

This was no more than a moment's grace, briefer than the telling. And in an airport, forsooth—the world's least likely place!

•

How the Jesuits cling in the mind! Strangely, and not always consolingly. Meeting them in the most diverse conditions and circumstances, from the university to the remote barrios, touched me to the quick. It was as though they held in hand a burning glass—focused on me. And what I saw reflected in that glass was someone who undoubtedly dwells in this world, but someone who was brought for a moment home to me—a news made new, welcome at once. Something of myself, the outsider and insider. The discomfort of living as I do, wanting to and not wanting to, grateful for the freedom hard won, conscious of how I use and abuse that freedom. Longing at time for the old rules of the game, the boundaries, the common observance unquestioningly followed. . . .

•

While I was in prison in the early seventies, one superior was wont to explain to the brethren, variously puzzled or angered at my delicts, that I was "in the society, but not of it." Quite possibly he was hitting a nail squarely. Or possibly not.

•

In light of such an event (or in its darkness), one is led to ask questions, a painful boon. As in the present circumstance. E.g.:

By what means, impelled by what events or circumstances, did so close a sense of spiritual fraternity arise among Jesuits in Central America? The question, I believe, can be raised without odium. It is not raised, I hasten to add, in an unqualified or merely romantic way, as though a meeting with such men, sensing the quality of their lives and work, their supportive love for one another, would not of itself lead to other questions, serious ones indeed.

•

"In the society, but not of it." It was, I recall, a cruel stripe to belabor me with, given the durance vile in which I passed my days and nights. Appearing as he did from time to time in the visitors' room at Danbury prison, the superior was disinclined to explain his terminology to me; in his eyes I had evidently passed from a subject of discussion or perplexity to a mere object of such.

Description, I thought, without consultation; taxation, so to speak, and no representation. Tyranny?

•

Let nostalgia roll. I sing the "dear dead days beyond recall."

I sing the days of cassock and biretta, of long black lines, of vow celebrations and threnodies at graveside ("Benedictus Deus Israel," that quintessential farewell of the priestly tribe to one of "ours"), days of public confessions and kissing of feet and taking meals on one's knees.

Farewell to the famous "Fourteen Points of the Manifestation of Conscience to Be Made to the Superior at Time of Renovation of Vows!" Farewell to the rustling rosary at one's side, to the great tintinabulum at dawn, to the whish! whish! of the rope discipline across bare shoulders, to the chain applied tightly to the thigh on rising from cot. . . .

Farewell to Father Master, his imperial outbursts (testing, testing!) the opening ploy of the game called "formation"; farewell also to Father Instructor, his gallic equanimity, his face a very moon of kindness (the last inning of the game, some fifteen years later . . .).

An altogether unregretful farewell to Anonymous Censors of Books, also to Authorized Openers of Mail, as well as to Virtuous Tattlers, hot on the trail, improving You Know Who. . . .

A dimissorial wave also to the three day Read-Ins of the Letters of the Fathers General, more especially those of the excoratory or fulminatory variety. Also, and with infinite relief, the striking of the fetters of auditory servitude; farewell to pulpit malpractice, to wit: Marian sermons, Sacred Heart sermons, annual blue-ribbon Greek sermons, semiannual Latin sermons. Also, passim throughout the year, and causative of later and permanent digestive ills: Sanguinary Martyrologies, Great Moments of the Order, Hammerings of Heretics. . . .

Farewell to Letters from Rome on occasion of this or that malificent tendency (worldliness, worldliness); farewell to those minatory missives, like a black frown on a death mask: *O tempora! O mores!*

All gone, all gone; the life of the long house, the rule of the officers' club, the womb to tomb security. . . .

Was it Pirandello who disguised an angel as a train switchman and had him say to a group of befuddled exiles: "You're on your own, you know, no god at your service. . . . "

We're on our own; we've joined, like it or not, the common mode. Decisions are in our own hands and one takes his chances—deciding what seems best (or least awful) at the time, after weighing things, pro and con, and especially, beyond all calculation after weighing whether a decision fits one's tradition, a tradition that includes obedience (and something more), community (and something beyond).

Maybe the elusive more, the beyond, is the pressure of the tradition itself? (Maybe what we named tradition had been housebroken and tamed, a cultural convenience?) Hadn't Ignatius hinted at such danger, implying as he did in the first sentences of his rule that rules were redundant in proportion as Jesuits hearkened to the Spirit. . . . Holy Spirit or unholy, how was one to know?

In the act, the choice, one might be granted to know, after prayer, the prayer of Gethsemane, sweating it out. And then, one chose, it was simple as that. No need to add: consequences followed. One took them in account, if not in stride. The overstepping, so to speak, that follows on understanding.

And one found himself in the terrain yclept Insecurity. ("National Insecurity"—I think of the phrase when I think of the Central American Jesuits.) Insecurity? As a vacation spot it is not recommended. Its climate is of unpredictable fire and ice; its landmarks are named Fallout, Consequence, Land's End. And once arrived, one is considered an alien or a displaced person or an illegal alien; there are in fact no other categories.

•

Maybe the mutuality we note among the Central American Jesuits has occurred simply because they have chosen to live an endangered life. One searches for clues. I have a sense that these Jesuits chose, at some time, to live in a clear and truthful way—as though the gospel were serious, as though they could also be serious about their faith, and its consequences.

The public situation, horrifying as it was in Nicaragua only a decade ago and horrible as it remains in Salvador, actually helped such decisions along, as was indicated to us in various ways.

One of them said: "We came to see that we must either stand together or we would perish." (And this was no mere gentleman's agreement or marriage of convenience, as their conduct and bearing made clear.)

•

TO THE JESUITS OF CENTRAL AMERICA: THE GRATITUDE OF A BROTHER

Some stood up once, and sat down.
   Some walked a mile, and walked away.

Some stood up twice, then sat down.
   I've had it, they said.

Some walked two miles, then walked away.
   It's too much, they said.

Some stood and stood and stood.
   They were taken for dunces
   They were taken for fools
   They were taken for being taken in.

Some walked and walked and walked.
  They walked the earth
  They walked the waters
  They walked the air.

Why do you stand?
they were asked, and
Why do you walk?

Because of the children, they said, and
Because of the heart, and
Because of the bread

Because
  the cause
  is the heart's beat
  and the children born
  and the risen bread.

•

Managua, June 21. Saint Luis Gonzaga. My thirty-second anniversary of ordination. Were he living, my father's one hundred fifth birthday. Carol's birthday. Elizabeth stands convicted in Syracuse for antinuclear activity.

Our scattered clan: in Italy, in Central America, in and out of jail, dwelling in this world and in eternity. . . .

Will someone please tell me how we might learn to walk in step, to "do our thing," to let sleeping dogs lie, to stop making waves? It must be admitted, we're close to unteachable. Worse, we rejoice in our plight, take perverse pleasure in it.

Theologically, this is probably considered a dangerous state. Juridically, it places us beyond rehabilitation.

•

Anniversaries! A time to launch into the empyrean, to proclaim immortal, edifying thoughts, messages, manifestos to humanity, last wills and ever-newer testaments, sublime words to be sealed in time capsules, an absolutely irrefutable roundup of the human scene!

The above is, of course, the veriest balderdash. One's best response to such a day is a chastened prayer that the past offered, in spite of all, slightly less ill than good, that the future might be equally, ever-so-slightly favored. For the rest, one faces the world wearing a half-shamed grin, as at the commission of a blooper before a distinguished assembly. . . .

•

According to today's *La Prensa,* the archbishop of Managua summons the people, in face of continuing government attacks on the church, to a "renewed loyalty." The phrase is troublesome, ambiguous—possibly because it is secular to the core, applied to the church only at risk of odium. . . . One may well be "loyal" to Caesar; toward the church, one had best strive to be faithful. The rub is that loyalty brooks no criticism, allows of no second thoughts before this or that edict. And deprived of such, the church inevitably becomes secular as hell. A church resembling a state, one that can inspire and demand only loyalty oaths. A fascist church, finally, composed of lockstepping members.

•

Two hours late, our plane arrives in driving rain. Departure for Miami is announced. I shoulder my backpack—hesitations, queries, doubts (and then two or three convictions, the heaviest burden of all). For such considerable luggage, I reflect wryly, one should pay an overweight charge of passage.

5
Envoi

Inedible food is one of the few truly international offerings of the age. TACA Airlines, to prepare us for re-entry in the free world, served an abominable meal between Nicaragua and Miami. The omniplastic quality was relieved somewhat by the presence on my tray of a disconsolate carnation. Its spirit was broken, no doubt, by being required to survive in this air, in contrariety to its nature. I whispered verses of the Song of Songs to its ear. But it was not comforted.

•

Miami from the southland. What memories! In 1965, against all expectation, and contrary to the prevailing winds (the ecclesiastically acceptable war in Vietnam, the sedulous military Cardinal), I was summoned home after exile in Latin America. It is perhaps allowed, therefore, that a vagrant tear fall softly on the pall of memory!

Given the stereophonic world of Latin America, and the scant and hurried four months of my previous sojourn there, I may well have seen too much too quickly in 1965. Perhaps. In any case, I recall that, impenitent on return as on departure, in nowise rendered tractable, I was ready for more. . . .

•

Today I would be a fonder fool than report allows, were I to think that easy answers were at hand to the questions these weeks have raised.

What, indeed, of the priests, their government posts, their party memberships, their high responsibilities for policy? The question is by no means settled by a high-minded sneer in the direction of Rome. Rome could take a far less rigid position, and the questions would remain, biblical questions not so much of church discipline (in which terms the curia and pope commonly couch them), but questions of sacrament and tradition.

In the calculus of worldly power, a cynical arithmetic assumes that two evils cancel each other out. But one can hardly yield to such perverse logic, assuming one loves both the church and our Nicaraguan priests.

•

In contrast, I reflect that mine has been a far easier way. Whether by circumstance or temperament, I have never been required by life to cope with the tornadoes of power or wildly spinning vane of public life. I could well depart this world on command, content to have salvaged at least a recognizable portion of my humanity; no great mover and shaker, grateful that life placed no large burdens on a creaky frame.

And yet, and yet, all this said, we do not lay vexing questions to rest by declaring that the questions do not touch us. . . . When we sat in that eerie shed among the gritty militia in Ocotal, or when in Managua certain suppositions were placed implicitly beyond question (by priests who, as makers of public policy, were agreeable to suspend their sacrament and word for the duration), I confess that before such I became profoundly uneasy.

I felt a tightening of the gut. Some capital point was being underscored in my presence; the point once made, the point of view once taken for granted—it followed that other points were to be ignored as irrelevant in the real world.

•

The "real world" is, alas, often enough a place we choose to label as such. It includes a populace exploding with fears, violence, obsessions, selfish ideologies, a "security system" that creates havoc as its chief export—to other worlds.

Real world? There is a planetary system of worlds labeled "real": capitalist real, Marxist real, first, second, and third world real. They orbit one another uneasily; they are in near collision, and the outcome sets the stoutest hearts to trembling.

The real world? Who is to name it or inhabit it? We set sail due east, we say, like enchanted Columbuses. But all our maps are wrong. We voyage due west. A continent looms up; it is in our way, we fret. So we land where we would not. We beach in a world; enchanted and self-deceived, as we are, we label it the "wrong one. . . ."

Another image occurs. In a space shot, the surest way to miss the moon is to set course directly toward it. It is the long way round, the way of trial and imagination and parabola, that touches on the unknown. . . .

•

In Ocotal, I asked myself in considerable confusion of spirit: What indeed am I to learn in a place where, two weeks previously, blood was exacted from enemy and defender, combatant and bystander? Am I to approve or condemn or to be silent and suspend all judgment, believing as I do that killing begets killing, that guns in whatever hands are under the judgment of the Gospel? . . .

And what of the Nicaraguan priest who shows abroad a film depicting the military training of new recruits, one scene of which concerns the use of arms? At each volley the name of a Somozan is shouted, presumably the target of revolutionary fervor. . . .

I am reasonably certain that every priest I met assumed the "right of just defense," understood as the right to maim or kill or otherwise repel the oppressor, torturer, dictator, contra. And this, though such a right can nowhere be found vindicated in our Gospel. The priests, moreover, work in the realm of official ideology and policy, which one of them described to me as "that realm of lies."

With such questions and doubts and a few convictions, I wing northward, into the Land of Unknowing.

•

> We believe in history;
> the world is not a roll of dice,
> a bet on chaos.

ENVOI

A new world has begun
since Christ has risen.
Jesus, we rejoice in your triumph!
Beyond the crushing of our lives
has begun an eternal alleluia!
From the thousand wounds
of bodies and souls
a triumphant song!
Teach us to give voice
to new life in the world
because you dry the tears of the oppressed
and death shall be no more.

Luis Espinal, S.J.
+ 1980

Also by Daniel Berrigan

PROSE

The Bride: Essays in the Church
The Bow in the Clouds
Consequences, Truth and
Love, Love at the End
They Call Us Dead Men
Night Flight to Hanoi
No Bars to Manhood
The Dark Night of Resistance
America Is Hard to Find
The Geography of Faith (with Robert Coles)
Absurd Convictions, Modest Hopes (with Lee Lockwood)
Jesus Christ
Lights on in the House of the Dead
The Raft Is Not the Shore (with Nhat Hanh)
A Book of Parables
Uncommon Prayer: A Book of Psalms
Beside the Sea of Glass: The Song of the Lamb
The Words Our Savior Taught Us
The Discipline of the Mountain
We Die Before We Live
Portraits, of Those I Love
Ten Commandments for the Long Haul
The Nightmare of God

POETRY

Time Without Number
No One Walks Waters
Encounters
The World for Wedding Ring
False Gods, Real Men
Trial Poems (with Tom Lewis)
Prison Poems
Selected and New Poems
May All Creatures Live
Journey to Block Island

DRAMA

Trial of the Catonsville Nine